FROM
FAT FARM
TO
PHAT FARM

Edited by Mary Anne Christiano
Co-edited by Diara Rivera
Nutritional edited by Natalie Menza
Cover shot by David Capri

To order additional copies of this book, contact:
Xlibris Corporation
1-888-795-4274
www.Xlibris.com
Orders@Xlibris.com
90847

FROM FAT FARM TO PHAT FARM

Never Give Up!

Karim Ramos

"I felt so inspired and motivated after I heard Karim's story that I wanted to be apart of this project. So many of us can relate to him and what he has been through. Thank you for speaking for the voices that can't be heard. Continue to inspire and motivate, Karim. The transition you over came physically, emotionally, and mentally deserves to be heard."

Victor Martinez
IFBB Arnold Classic Champion 2007 & 2nd Runner Up Mr. Olympia 2007

I dedicate this book to my family. Guys, please understand, I love you with all my heart and would give my life for you all. This book is based on how I saw things from my eyes growing up in the Ramos' home.

Dad, thank you for all the blessed lessons. You were hard on my brother, my sisters, and me and I understand why . . . You wanted to make us the best we could be . . . thank you. I love you and admire so many things about you. I pray that if and when I have children, they do as I did and learn from the good and bad as I did with you, father. You taught me to be responsible and make sure to provide for my family. I am proud to have you in my life.

Mom (Mami), yo te amo tanto mami . . . gracias por todo lo que has hecho en mi vida. I love you, mom! Your baby boy has written his first book! I know when I first told you about this project, you didn't really understand what I was doing. Mom this is my life in a book, how I see it. You have always been there for me from day one. No matter how imperfect I was and am, you are always right there to kiss my head and tell me everything will be okay. You've always had a sixth sense for things I couldn't see. Mom, I thank you for teaching me how to love and the importance of a heart. I am sorry you didn't get the life you deserved to live, but I promise I will do everything in my power to give it to you before the end of time . . . Get ready to go on vacation with your baby boy. I love you, mami. No other woman will have your touch.

Cheyenne, we did it, bro! Chayi, just know that I admire you. thank you for always being my super hero and saving my life . . . I wouldn't be here if it wasn't for you.

Yassina and Yazmin, enjoy the book, guys. I'm sure it will bring back many memories . . . I love you two!

Thalia, Yaneris, Gianni, and Yanna I love you, guys and I hope that after you read this book, you will want to be better than me . . . . You guys are a blessing in my life. REMEMBER to be there for each other and love each other . . . Family is all you have at the end of the day.

Russell Simmons and Rev. Run, thank you for welcoming me to the family and giving me a place in your hearts. Thank you for also giving me your blessings on this book project.

Myorr, thank you for being like a big brother to me, and MOST of all, for giving me a shot at working for you with no college degree. You helped me change from a boy to a man and I appreciate all the many lessons.

Thank you to Myorr Janha, Kate Kuykendall, Victor Martinez, Joseph DeAcetis, Steve Lobel, Rasheed Young, Bel Todmann, Kev "Dogg" Jones, Serci Janha, Jasmine Sanders, Jody Miller, Charles Poole, Rod Carrera, Bianca Cartagena, Diara Rivera, Natalie Menza, Nick Freglette, Rachel Harriet, Mike Cusamano, Ang White, Laurie Joy, Sandra Correa, Bobby Alvino, T.U.F.F. Combat Threadz and everybody else I left out; I am sorry. I thank you for all the love and support you have given me throughout the last two years of doing this project. It's time to help those in need!

CONTENTS

Chapter 1   Memories 13

Chapter 2   The News 23

Chapter 3   When It Rains, It Pours 30

Chapter 4   The Road to Risk 42

Chapter 5   A "PHAT" Prayer Was Answered 51

Chapter 6   It Was All a Dream 56

Chapter 7   Play Your Position 75

Chapter 8   Oh So Focused 81

Chapter 9   The Sky's the Limit 87

Chapter 10   Health & Fitness Come First 96

Intro

"God put me on earth to help and serve him and those in need. No matter how famous, how much money, or poor you are, remember your roots. You're here for a purpose—mine is to serve. If you don't like it, then we know your purpose." Karim Ramos

I remember in 2008 I was in Jersey City, New Jersey, at a small corner store, picking up some snacks. I was standing in line to pay for my items and in front of me there was a woman paying for her food. With her were her two little children who both looked around 7 years old. The cashier said, "Miss, your total is $107.50." The lady looked embarrassed and said, "I'm sorry. I only have 83 dollars. Can I please take some stuff out of the cart?" Her children started taking their one little toy out as she started taking out toilet paper and wipes and canned food. I stopped her and said, "Please, don't do that." I looked at the cashier and I told her to put her tab on my tab combined and that I would pay for her. The lady kept saying, "No, no, no . . . please don't do this, you don't have to." but I insisted and told her to make sure her kids get the toys they want and I wanted her to put her money away. The lady cried a single tear and hugged me. It felt amazing doing such a good deed. As I was walking out of the store, the same lady was standing outside waiting for me, so I stopped and asked, "Are you okay?"

She looked at me and said, "You have no idea what an angel you are . . . .

"You have no idea what an angel you are . . . God is going to give you the biggest gift of your life for all the sacrifices and changes you have made. You are not supposed to be here, you're supposed to be famous, but you have so many people who wish bad on you and do not want to see you succeed. You will break through all the negative people in your life and you are going to change the world with your words on paper. Trust me, you will change the way they think and act out of nature, your heart will be heard across the world and you will change so many people. You are an angel! Thank you for helping me and my children in a time of need."

Now I know what she meant . . . .

CHAPTER 1

Memories

"Life isn't about where you start, but better yet, where you are going. Just remember the journey of life you took to get where you are today. Appreciate the hard times as much as the good times. Never forget there is someone out there who has it worse than you." Karim Ramos

I was born in Bayamon, Puerto Rico, on August 11, 1980. Within a year my family moved to Ocala, Florida. We lived in a little old trailer in the middle of an open field. My father used to always say, "It doesn't matter how big or small a house is, but the people inside of it make it a home." My home consisted of my parents, my older brother Cheyenne and my two older sisters Yassina and Yazmin, and I was the baby. We always did everything as a family. It was like a Spanish version of the *Brady Bunch* except we never had a lot of money. We eventually moved into a small house about five miles away from the old trailer.

Growing up in the Ramos house, things were pretty good, but could also be pretty bad. My father was a strict and stubborn man who always had us kids doing chores on the weekends. My father's rules were: you could only get A's and B's on your report cards, no fighting with your family, and make sure the house is clean. I remember my father hitting me for every cigarette bud he found outside that I missed when I cleaned the front and back yard.

I remember seeing my father every morning while he was drinking the coffee my mother made him. She would iron his clothes and make his breakfast while he was in the shower. After Dad dressed and ate, that was it. We didn't see him all day long. During this time my father was working for a fire truck manufacturing company. It was the best job for us kids because Dad would come home in a different fire truck and let us play on it. He would show us the cool lights and sirens and all the kids in the neighborhood would come over to see it.

When I was six years old we all wanted to be singers like our father, so my dad used to record us on his 8-Track player. It always started with the oldest first. Cheyenne would go first and record with dad, then Yassina, then Yazmin, then me. As kids we grew up on Spanish & Oldies, almost like our parents tried to keep us away from any other kind of music. We would record for hours. My father was no "Joe Jackson", but he definitely wanted perfection, so as kids we all tried not to let him down.

We realized Yassina did not have the vocals to sing, so my father then worked with Cheyenne, Yazmin, and myself. We would all record together at night, but could see that Dad wanted Yazmin to be the "famous" one. He said that we would be a group and that Yazmin was going to be the lead singer. It shocked me that he didn't want Cheyenne to be the lead singer. Cheyenne had an incredible voice. Yazmin on the other hand, till this day, sounds just like Mariah Carey.

My father ended up buying us a Karaoke machine at a garage sale. When my family would leave me at home with my mom, I would sneak and practice on it. As I hit record to sing without music you could always hear my mother screaming in the background, "Karim Amed Ramos! Get off your father's machine before he kills you!"

At that age I just didn't listen because I grew a love for music. I would watch the Michael Jackson videos, and pretend I was him, but then again what kid didn't want to be like Michael Jackson? So I would sing, record, and play it back for hours, until my dad, sisters and brother got back home. By the time I was 7 years old I was telling everyone I wanted to be a famous singer, but my father had other plans for me. You see because I was heavier than most kids my age, my hands were also bigger, so dad wanted me to be a boxer. So I ran around and said I was the singing boxer!

I noticed my father started recording more with Yazmin than with Cheyenne and me. So I just recorded on the side when my dad was at work. My sisters and brother used to tell on me because I would use the karaoke machine without permission, so my dad would hit me and send me to my room. I would then grab a little tape recorder I got from my friend and record myself on that until dad wanted me to record with my brother and sister again. That didn't happen often so I just recorded alone in my room.

I grew a different passion for music as I started listening to the actual message singers were sending out in their songs. Being raised in a family that loved music and loved to sing, kind of made me intimidated, especially singing next to Cheyenne. He had so many talents. When Cheyenne would sing we would all stop and just listen. I saw the passion in Cheyenne's face and heard his passion for music in his voice. But Dad never really acknowledged Cheyenne for some reason; he wanted Yazmin to be the singer. I know this bothered Cheyenne a lot. My love for music only grew over the years. I always loved singing and I would always make songs up off the top of my head. I used to just "freestyle" and come up with my own words to other artists beats. I had a passion for music.

Things weren't always so great in my household. Sometimes I sit back and reflect on how my father raised us. I have always questioned his discipline. I just felt like it was a thin line to abuse. One day I will never forget was my last time adding salt to my food. It all happened when I was seven years old and was having breakfast with my mom and dad. I was pouring salt on my eggs and my dad said, "Karim, don't put too much salt because you're not going to eat it."

I still added the salt and began to eat, but didn't finish. Next thing I knew, Dad grabbed my face, pulled my head back, facing my mouth to the ceiling. He then squeezed my mouth open. He told me that since I had added all that salt to my food, he wanted me to eat all of it! Then, he took the top off the saltshaker and poured the entire contents down my throat. He slammed my mouth shut and told me to swallow the salt! The salt burned my throat as tears rolled down my face. My mother was yelling at my father, begging him to let me go. Finally, Dad released my face and with the burning feeling in my throat, I started vomiting in the sink and bleeding out of my nose.

I never added salt to my food again.

When I was about 9 years old my family went to my aunt's house for dinner. My dad was cutting a watermelon and it was so delicious that I kept asking for another slice. By the time I got to the third piece, he looked down at me and slapped me in the face with the knife. "Stop asking me for another slice. The answer is no!" he said, "and don't you dare cry."

I looked at him, took a deep breath and headed to the bathroom, where I cried alone. You see, my father really didn't have the patience to deal with me. And I don't hate him at all. I have a wonderful connection with my dad today. I know a lot of you would probably grow up resenting him. I did for a while, but then you have to realize you can either grow up with hatred in your heart or with love. It's up to you.

My father was a hustler. You could never take that away from him. Dad was and still is the type of man that comes out with the best ideas and new ways to make a lot of money. The only problem was that he never followed through with about 99 percent of them. He has always been admired and respected by everyone he encountered. He taught so many people many things about life. I can't even count the amount of times someone has come up to me and said, "Your father is a genius, Karim, you're so fortunate to have this great wise man in your life." It made me feel so good to hear that. My father fought in Vietnam for the Air Force and I can remember as a child he did so much to provide for his family. He went from sales to marketing for a business to then working at the fire truck manufacturing company. My father now holds an important position as a Federal Law Enforcement officer. He climbed the ladder of success and I admire him and realized in life it's not where you are, but where you are going.

My dad never showed any real emotion when it came to us kids. I remember as a small boy around the age of five I would sneak into my parents' room and lay down on the floor next to my mother so I could hold her hand while I sleep. Of course I'd rather lie in the bed but my father didn't like that. I would lie next to her side of the bed, reach my hand up and she would kiss my hand and hold it until I fell asleep. Then she would put my hand back on the ground so my hand wouldn't fall asleep from poor circulation.

One of the many lessons my father always taught us was, "One man's junk is another man's treasure." We were very used to garage sales, yard sales, and Salvation Armies. My father never really believed in buying new things. From beds, clothes, sneakers, to house furniture, everything was used . . . everything. I can remember the time my father forgot I had picture day at school and I had no decent sneakers to wear. Dad took my sisters sneakers that were pink and white, grabbed the cleaning spray, and cleaned them. He then handed me the sneakers and said, "Here you go." So I went to my fifth grade photo shoot with a pair of my sister's pink and white sneakers. This was one of my most embarrassing moments ever.

I remember when it came to school grades I was the only one, out of the four kids in my family, to get bad grades. My brother and sisters were averaging good grades and I was averaging bad ones. As a child for some reason I couldn't focus, like I had ADD or something. When I was in first grade I remember the teacher asking me, "Karim, what do you do when you're home?"

I responded, "Sleep and eat."

Soon after that conversation my parents were called in and informed that the school was putting me back in kindergarten. So, I went back a grade for being honest. I just couldn't grasp learning the boring things they were teaching me in class. For this reason my dad punished and spanked me a lot. It got to the point that on Report Card Day I was crying the moment I would walk home from the bus stop. Even my brother Cheyenne, nicknamed "Chayi," would lose patience trying to teach me my times tables and would yell at me. I felt like an idiot. I really had a hard time learning.

My father and I were never really close. I feared him. My love for him when I was young was out of fear. I don't blame him. I blame the man that raised him, his father. My father was firm with all of us kids and he always expected so much from my brother Chayi because he was the leader of the pack. We never knew that one day my father's high expectations would back fire in his face years later. While my father was strict and distant, it was Cheyenne that I looked up to. Chayi was favored and loved by everyone. He was flawless. He was athletic, playing all sports from soccer to football to track. My brother was even an altar boy at our local church. He was definitely an "All American."

One day I was about six years old, I remember Chayi and I playing outside. My oldest sister, Yassina, came to us crying, that the kid across the street was picking on her. Chayi yanked my hand and said, "Let's go do something about this, Kari."

I didn't know what to say, but since my big brother was mad, I was mad too. So we walked across the street and my brother picked up a frog and handed it to me and said, "Kari, hold the frog in your hands and don't drop it."

We approached Jason's house and my brother said, "Hey Jason, don't you dare mess with my sister ever again!"

Chayi pushed Jason to the ground and started fighting him! I didn't know what to do, so I did exactly what my brother asked me to do, which was holding on to the big frog for as long as I could. Then my brother grabbed Jason's arms and legs and wouldn't let him get out of the hold.

"Kari, take the frog and shove it in his mouth," Cheyenne said. "Put it in his mouth and squeeze his mouth and nose together until he swallows it!"

I was nervous and confused because my brother just asked me to shove a live frog in a kid's mouth!

"Do it now, Kari! Nobody messes with our family."

While Jason was crying and screaming, I opened his mouth and slammed the frog in his mouth and squeezed his mouth and nose as tight as I could. Then I started yelling, "This is for my sister!" as Jason swallowed the frog!

Cheyenne let him go and said, "If you ever pick on anybody in our family again, I will make you swallow something worse." Jason just looked at us like we were crazy.

Another great unforgettable moment with Cheyenne is around the same time when I was about seven and Cheyenne was fourteen years old. We went walking into the swamps in Florida pretending to be in the army looking for trees to climb. Well Cheyenne came across a very big egg near the lake. He grabbed a stick, called me over to him, and started poking the egg. I grabbed another stick and started poking it too. Before you know it we heard a deep growl from the distance. I look over my shoulder and asked Chayi if he heard what I heard. Cheyenne said yes. As we poked the egg again to see what it was we heard the growl get closer and closer to us. The vibration under our feet moved viciously towards our way. Cheyenne looked up, paused for a second and grabbed me. He pushed me forward and said, "RUNNNNN!"

I ran not knowing what I was running from. As we were running, Cheyenne said, "Kari, run diagonally! Run, run, run!"

I looked back at Cheyenne and I saw an Alligator chasing us! I screamed for my life and felt the panic in my heart! Cheyenne screamed, "Climb up the tree, Kari!" I ran faster and faster, with Cheyenne right behind me. I could see the alligator getting closer and closer to us. Cheyenne quickly climbed the tree first then grabbed me and pulled me up to him. The alligator missed my feet by inches. My brother grabbed me and said he was sorry for scaring me He squeezed me and begged me not to tell Mom or Dad, or even our sisters. I kept my promise. We looked down at the alligator as it waited for us to climb down the tree. We got home that night five hours passed dinner time. My father was upset with us and he spanked and punished us both. Cheyenne and I now shared a secret and we learned a lesson that day . . . . Respect Mother Nature.

But while Cheyenne was always there for me when we were children, we drifted apart as we grew a little older. My brother had no time for me. It was all about him working on music with his friends, his girlfriends, sports, and school. My brother was so incredible he could do two different homework assignments at the same time. He would work on one with his left hand and use his right hand for the other! Come on, how could I compare to that? I'd have to do my homework with my feet to compete with that.

I remember Cheyenne always being the center of attention and I would sit back and see how proud my father was of him while my sisters and mother all favored him. I felt like an outsider. I felt like the "ugly duckling." My love for my brother developed into jealousy and envy. I wanted that life. I wanted to be him. I wanted my family to actually say, "Karim we are so proud of you." But that was just merely wishful thinking. Cheyenne was indestructible and I was just self-destructible.

Cheyenne was the good guy and I was the bad guy. I did everything wrong. I had to hear from my mother, father, and sisters, "Why can't you be more like Cheyenne?" Life moved on and Cheyenne was just living life better and better and I was getting fatter and fatter. My brother was winning awards at school and getting paid scholarships to different universities while I was eating food as my getaway from reality. Growing up in my brother's shadow, of his perfections made me more insecure and less confident in myself as a child.

With Cheyenne no longer in the picture to protect me because he was too busy with his life, kids in school started to pick on me. They picked on me for having big ears, being chubby, and even for the gap in my teeth. My gap tooth was big as a child and I can remember my father saying I could eat corn through a picket fence. Because of my big ears, kids would flick them and call me Dumbo. Even when I got to middle school I had kids tease and torment me.

I had no friends. My brother was too old to want to take his little brother around with him, so I'd hang out with my sisters, who started referring to me as "Karimcita", referring me to a girl because I had no guy friends. One day I had enough, and went crying to my mother. I told her what Yassina and Yazmin were calling me. Mom immediately grabbed me by my sides, picked me up, and put me on top of the counter top. She called my sisters over and asked them, "Do you have this?"

And she pulled my pants down, flashing my sisters! I was so embarrassed but I stuck my little chest out, proud as can be. My sisters screamed. And my mother said,

"Stop calling him girl names because he's a man!"

Although they learned their lesson that day, it didn't stop them in the future. Even though I fought with my sisters, they were there for me when I needed them. One day a kid named Zack pushed me off my bike. I fell to the pavement and as I was getting up, he asked, "What are you going to do, fat boy?" I was stunned because this kid was fatter than me! I simply ran home, crying. My mom asked what happened and I never answered. But Yassina and Yazmin were watching from down the block. They took me by the hand and walked me down to Zack's house. They grabbed Zack, held him down and told me to hit him. I was kicking and punching, but in the wrong direction! Here I was saying, "Here it comes! Yeah, it's going to hurt!"

My sisters let go of Zack, grabbed my hands and started walking me back home. "Kari, why were you fighting the air? Loser!" one of them said.

I replied, "Hey, I don't know how to fight!"

The teasing was relentless from age 11, onward. I was in a bubble of torture. I didn't like how I looked and felt. It was crazy how scared I got from the physical and mental abuse. I would be the fat kid who didn't want to take his shirt off at the pool. I would pray someone pushed me in the water so I could just swim.

Among all the harassment, I was in the shadow of Cheyenne Ramos who was now modeling at the age of 18. Each morning I woke up in a world that I felt was the end. In a world where I felt alone and was just standing on the sidelines while everyone else just smiled. We have some good memories as children, but why do we hold on to the bad ones? Why do the bad outweigh the good? I tried to hold on to the good memories, but I couldn't. In my mind and in my heart, I was scared. I always wondered where I would be in my life at the age of twenty-five . . . would I be alive??

Me & Dad

Me & Dad

Me & Mom

Me & Mom before my Junior Prom

Yassina, Me & Yazmin

CHAPTER 2

The News

"Learn from yesterday, live for today, and prepare for tomorrow." Karim Ramos

My mother Luz, also known as Lucy, was the complete opposite of my dad. She was the soft spot in my life. No matter what I did or said, she could only be mad at me for a short time before she was letting me play again or giving me a hug or kiss. My grandparents on my mother's side were also the opposite of the grandparents on my father's side. My grandmother, known as Abuela, was a sweet, small, woman who died from a heart attack when I was 18. My grandfather was a pleasant man also, but died very shortly after Abuela. He was actually missing her so much that he was hallucinating that she was still alive and would call her name and look for her in the house. I guess when you're so in love, and a part of you dies, you have no choice but to go too.

While Mom was not the best advice giver when it came to finances or life in general, she was the best when it came to love and affection. Dad was more the financial advisor, the one you could turn to for guidance on work. Sometimes there was an equal balance. Dad was the worker and mom was the stay-at-home mom. Dad asked mom to stay home and take care of the kids while he worked so she did. My mother was like a queen in my eyes. As a child I knew she would be my best friend, someone I could talk to and confide in. She always lectured me on the importance of treating people right and respecting women. Mom definitely gave me my heart and emotions but my dad on the other hand was cold and not affectionate at all. When you are young, you always think your parents are built for each other.

I remember at the age of 13, my parents called everyone to the kitchen. It must have been the scariest tone of voice I've ever heard my father call us in. It wasn't the "normal" tone. It actually sounded more sympathetic. Something must have been wrong.

I was sitting on a stool, at the center, next to my dad. Cheyenne was standing at the door that leads towards the back yard. Yassina was standing next to Mom, and Yazmin, on the other side of Dad and me. Dad looked at all of us, with a look we didn't recognize, and said, "Kids, we called you here to tell you that your mother and I do not love each other anymore and we're getting separated."

"Tell them why," my mother said.

"Lucy, we do not love each other and that's it! Kids, we have decided that it is just not going to work anymore," responded Dad.

I think my siblings and I all felt the same way—speechless. I felt my heart crack in half. Everything we did as a family, all our weekends of laughter, all our arguments, all happy, sad and stressed times were thrown down the drain. Everything we stood for as a family, everything my father preached to us was just a waste of words. My brother started crying and then we all started crying. Our parents continued to express to us that it was not our fault and that they just did not share that love for each other anymore.

Life was at its end when we heard the news. So much ran through our heads. What happens next? What happens to us? Do I ever get to see my family together in one room again? Is this my fault for being so immature and always trying to get into trouble? The days of hearing my mother and fathers laughter in the same room were at an end. The only thing I could do at 13 years old was stay out of my parents' way. I felt like everything my father preached to me as a child, about how important a family was, was dead and long gone. I remember asking my brother what he was going to do about the horrible news. He looked at me and said, "There's nothing I can do." So I left my parents divorce in God's hands and let Him take control of the situation.

From that day on, I noticed a difference in my brother's attitude, goals, and personality. Cheyenne ended up joining the United States Marine Corp. When he left me and the family, it was so quiet and lonely. I constantly wrote to him and he'd write back, but when he came out of the Marines, he was a complete different guy. He had no fear in his eyes or any feeling in his heart.

My sisters, my mother, and I ended up moving back to Ocala, FL, while my father stayed in New Jersey with my brother, to continue his career in federal law enforcement. After 25 years of marriage, my mother packed up and left without her husband. We had no father with us. My dad became a "parking lot father"—a man that comes by to see his kids in a parking lot, and then goes his way. The house we moved into was small and it got harder and harder for my mom to raise a family as a single parent. Ever since she met my father, she never worked because my father wanted her to be a "stay at home mother and housewife." My mother had a college degree and had her path made for her career until she met my dad.

Mom stayed home and served my father for 25 years because that's what my father wanted. My mother played the position of an old school wife, who served her husband and respected his wishes. Now here came the day she found herself applying for a factory job in Florida, sewing uniforms, the day she never thought she'd see. It was a slave driven job where you sit in a small factory with no heat or air conditioner. She was sewing uniforms for minimum wage. My father wasn't sending money for us or the bills on a regular basis. We had no idea why.

I remember one day I went to the store with my mother and she bought food for the house and I threw a Snickers bar in the cart. My mother went to the cashier, and as the clerk rang her up, I noticed she was counting money that looked like money from the game Monoploy. She was counting fake money! I asked her what that was and the clerk said, "Those are food stamps."

"What's a 'food stamp'?" I asked the clerk.

"Ask your mother," she said. So I did, but Mom just ignored me. Then I noticed Mom took out a real dollar bill to pay for my Snickers bar.

When we got in the car, I asked my mother what the fake money was for. She looked at me and said, "Son, if we want to eat, we have to use this fake money. I don't make enough money to pay the rent and bills for the house. But don't worry, Baby, it's only temporary."

I couldn't grasp a lot from that, except that we did not have money. So I went home and started knocking on doors in my neighborhood asking people to let me cut their lawns for ten bucks. I did that every weekend and before I knew it, I was doing it with a regular client list on Saturdays and Sundays. I was giving my money to my mom so she could use it for whatever she needed. My mother felt so guilty and would turn me away so I would just put it in her pocketbook. My father sent me twenty dollars in a birthday card and I gave that to my mom too. At the age of thirteen I had to do whatever I could to help mom.

Soon afterwards, we ended up back in New Jersey because my mother couldn't keep trying to take care of us, work *and* pay the bills on her own. She packed us up and moved us to my father's condo in Woodbridge, New Jersey, where he and my brother had been living. My mother was shocked to see how good my father had it! We were in Florida, barely having a roof over our heads, while my father bought a condo and never told my mother. When my father got home from work and saw all his kids in the house, with his ex-wife, his mouth dropped. My dad had to eventually move into a studio apartment in Fords, New Jersey, until my parents' divorce was finalized in court and my mother could receive money on a regular basis. In the mean while me, Mom, Cheyenne and my sisters were all living in a two-bedroom townhouse. But, hey, we had to struggle in order to stick it out together.

Things didn't go so well for us in this house. My sister Yassina ended up getting pregnant at 17. I was out in the streets at all times of the night and failing school. Cheyenne was working selling furniture and Yazmin was just attending high school. It was so bad and I was so confused on what was going on in our lives. I remember going to school and getting suspended for throwing my desk and chair at a kid who was talking about my mother. I know it was a dumb thing to do and I regret it. The worst thing about it was when I got home, my mother said the words that I was afraid of hearing: "Wait until your father sees you!"

When my "parking lot father" pulled up to the house, I can remember my heart pounding and palms sweating from nervousness. As I am walking to his car, I see him on the phone. The closer I get to the car, the more my heart starts pounding. I opened the door and sat down in the passenger seat. I was sitting there with my hands interlocked and just waiting for what was going to happen next. My father was still on the phone and as he's talking, I noticed he locked all the doors with a push of a button. My father said "good-bye" to whomever he was talking to, then, not even letting go of the phone, swings a fist to my face, followed by another punch to the face that slammed my head in the window again, followed by about five more punches.

I turned to him and screamed, "I'm sorry!"

He kept hitting me and said, "You think you're big and bad, I'll show you big and bad!" Punch after punch, until he was tired. He unlocked the doors and said, "Get out." I got out and walked back in the house. My mother asked what happened and I said, "Nothing." I went to my room and locked the door. I remember staring at myself in the mirror, wanting to kill my father because of the way he beat me. He treated me as though I was an enemy of his instead of his son. The look in his eyes as one fist came at me following by another fist was almost like a Rocky movie, except it wasn't acting. It was all reality. As I am putting toilet paper in my nose to stop the bleeding, I kept telling myself in the mirror, "He really does love you. This is all a lesson, Karim."

Months later, when it couldn't get worse, it did. In eight grade I performed a song at Iselin Middle School. It was our spring concert and I was at my after-party celebration because we had just performed. I performed a solo, "Earth Angel." The concert was great! It was a sold-out show and that was my first time realizing that I could really touch people's hearts and minds through my voice. I was sitting around with my chorus teacher and fellow students, enjoying the cake and compliments, when I looked up and saw the principal and two police officers coming my way. I had no idea why they were walking towards me and one of the police officers said, "Mr. Ramos, please come with us to the principal's office."

In my mind, I was like, *This has to be a joke.* So I took one more bite of my cake, and as I'm lifting the fork to my mouth, one of the officers grabbed my hand and made me let go of the cake. That's when I knew it was serious. I got to the principal's office and I asked her what happened. She looked at me and said, "You took it too far, Karim."

So sidetracked by what just happened, I asked, "What did I do?"

"Karim, you hit your English teacher!"

I was completely shocked and everything she said after that, I couldn't understand. I looked up at her with tears in my eyes and said, "Why would I ever do that?"

I explained to my principal that I was given a pass to see the nurse by my substitute teacher. My English teacher saw me in the hallway talking with a girl and she kept telling me to get to class (not knowing I was already going to see the nurse) so I went back to my classroom and told my substitute teacher that my English teacher was not letting me go to the nurse's office. As I was explaining to my substitute teacher, my English teacher came in, and not knowing she was standing right behind me, I turned my head to walk out and I hit her arm that was stretched across the doorway with my head.

My English teacher said, "Excuse you!" and I told her I was sorry, that I didn't know her arm was there.

She looked at me and said, "I thought so."

I looked at my substitute teacher and told her to please tell my English teacher I have a pass to go to the nurse's office. My English teacher looked at me and said the nurse's office is closed anyways. So I never even got the chance to see the nurse. And now I'm here, sitting with my principal who's expelling me for hitting a teacher, which is false and wrong! I told my principal to get the substitute teacher who saw everything.

My principal said, "Karim, I know you didn't really hit her and the substitute teacher and your fellow students all vouch for you, but your English teacher wants to take the school education system to court if I do not expel you. So three weeks prior to my 8th grade graduation, I was expelled for being at the wrong place at the wrong time. I remember getting escorted home with my principal and the two police officers. The principal made me translate to my mother what happened and that I was not going to be able to attend my 8th grade graduation and dance. My principal looked out for me in a way and said I could go to the 9th grade in the same school as my sister and that I did not have to do summer school.

Mother hit me and punished me. I was so afraid of my father punching me for being suspended so I begged Mom not to tell him. She told him, but made sure I didn't see him and he didn't see me. I remember my friends coming by my bedroom every couple of days and talking to me from the window. I felt like a prisoner. I couldn't even watch television. So, as I sat in my room depressed, I contemplated killing myself and ending the misery and the embarrassment I had caused my father, mother and my entire family. I started getting mad and upset that my mother kept me on punishment. I could hear my mother arguing with my sisters about how my father was not giving her enough money to buy food and things she needed in the house. My mother would tell my sisters, "Tell your father what he's giving me isn't enough, guys."

I sat in my room video recording myself every day, talking to the camera, saying that this will be my last video because I wanted to die. Then about a month later, I looked at the camera and said I was going to ask Mom if I could go to the store for her and she did. She wanted me to get her eggs. I walked down to a sandwich restaurant and asked if I could speak with the owner or manager. A man named Jason came out from the back room and I asked, "Sir, can I speak to you, please?"

He said, "Sure."

I sat with Jason at a table and said, "I want to work for you. I know I'm under age, and I still have a year before I can legally work for you, but I'll stay in the back, clean up, mop, take out the trash . . . whatever you want me to do, I'll do it."

Jason looked at me and asked, "Why should I hire you?"

I explained that I was alone, that I let my family down, that I wanted to give money to my mother to help out with food, that my school year was starting soon and I was tired of my father taking me and my sisters to the Salvation Army to get clothes for school. I wanted to buy my own stuff.

Jason smiled and said, "You're hired, Kiddo!"

I came home and told my mom I found a job making sandwiches making money under the table (not taxed). She was concerned because I was so young and it was illegal, so I said, "Mom, let me help you out with the money problems."

She looked at me with a look of embarrassment, but humble. She said, "Okay, Son, thank you."

I hugged her and said, "Mom, this is all temporary."

Before I knew it, I was working at the sandwich place seven days a week! I made sandwiches and helped run the store while all my friends talked trash and said I had no life because all I did was work during my summer vacation. I never told them I was making $10 an hour under the table. I was just stacking my money and helping Mom out with food.

Just before the new school year started, my father pulled up to the house to take my sisters and I to the Salvation Army, or to the little stores that sold bootleg cheap clothes. I told my father I didn't need him to take me. I told him to spend my half on my sisters. He was shocked and asked why. My sister told him I had been working all summer long. What an amazing feeling that was. I walked into the ninth grade with fresh kicks, new clothes, and jewelry on. I may have been fat, but I was "Fly". I remember as a kid my father taking me to the Salvation Army for school clothes, but here I was fourteen buying my own Nikes, Polo shirts, timberland boots, and jeans . . . AND still gave mom money to help her out. Later on things got too hectic. I was running track, playing football and wrestling, and singing in the chorus. I couldn't keep my job at the sandwich shop so I quit right after I cut my thumb on the slicing machine. I went to the hospital because I cut through my nail. That was my sign to quit.

Growing up in my teen years was so bad, I lost the sandwich job, but realized mom was still struggling with money. I was stealing from stores to give money to my mom. I didn't care how fat I was and I didn't care about grades in school. I felt like my family praised my brother because he was athletic, smart and good looking, and everyone wanted to hang out with him. I was tired of my family comparing me to him. I was tired of my "parking lot father" coming over to yell at me about grades or comparing me to my brother or my friends. I started hanging out with the thugs and not caring about where life went. The more I got yelled at, the more I kept deliberately getting in trouble. I would steal candy bars and toys, that kids would want, to sell them in school the next day. I made about two hundred dollars a week selling what I got for free! I would place money in my mother's purse without her knowing, and keep money for myself.

It was great until one day I was leaving the house and my mother asked me where I was going so late at night. I said, "I told you a million times, don't worry!"

I went to the store to steal some CDs and candy bars for some guys in school. As I was walking home from the mall I heard footsteps running closer to me. Right before I looked over my shoulder, I got punched in the back of my head, right in the center, knocking me out flat on my face! I turned over, onto my back, after I regained my sight and focus. As I turned over, someone picked me up by my throat and slammed me up against the fence and punched me in the face. I had no idea who it was at this point, because I still hadn't regained focus from the first punch in the back of my head. Flashbacks were coming to me and I could see my dad punching me in the face again and again like he did in the car before. After the third punch to the face, I saw who it was—Cheyenne!

I yelled at the top of my lungs, "Stop!"

He grabbed me and kept punching me. He said, "You want to disrespect your mother? You want to be a thug? You want to be big and bad and rob people and steal from stores?" He kept punching, then he threw me against a fence and said, "Go ahead, Kari, hit me! Punch me in the face. Go ahead, you know you want to. "Hit me, punk!" Even with all the anger inside, I couldn't do it. I couldn't hit my brother.

Cheyenne said, "You should be ashamed of yourself, stealing like this! Are you crazy? Do you want to go to jail? Your father and mother never taught you this lifestyle."

I said, "I guess I will never be as perfect as you, Cheyenne."

He shed a tear and walked away.

My mother came home the next day and saw me sleeping on the couch in the living room and couldn't recognize me when she first saw me because my face was so swollen, I was filled with knots all over from Cheyenne's fists. She grabbed me and asked, "Kari, what happened?"

I told her I got jumped, but Cheyenne said he did it. My mother started hitting my brother and asked him if he was trying to kill me. My brother said, "No, he needs to learn a lesson!"

My mother screamed, "Are you crazy, Cheyenne? This is not right either! Why do you guys have to solve it so violently?"

I got between them and said that I deserved it. Then I went to my room and grabbed my secret stash of cookies and ate the whole package. I sat down in front of the mirror and wanted to end my life. I felt so useless, a helpless fat kid with no morals, no goals, nothing. That's when I realized I was eating my problems away. When I was happy I ate and when I sad I ate. Food became part of my lifestyle not caring how fat I would get.

CHAPTER 3

When It Rains, It Pours

*"We walk down the road of life, not knowing the reason for
the things that happen to us . . . but, there REALLY
is a plan for us all . . . just believe." Karim Ramos*

It's 1998 and I am a junior in high school. My life really had no direction. I was failing in school, fighting with my family, feeling like an abandoned soul and hating how every time I looked over my shoulder, I was being compared to my brother.

My sister Yassina gave birth to my niece, Thalia. At this point Yassina was having issues with her boyfriend Yobbany, because Thalia was unexpected. Being that Yassina was only seventeen years old, a mere child who did not believe in abortion, she did what she thought was right as a human and as a mother. Yassina was very stubborn and tried raising Thalia alone but realized that she needed Yobbany. I knew Yassina didn't have any money and I felt as an uncle I had to step up to the plate and help her out. I didn't have any money for her to help her take care of Thalia, so I went back to my old ways . . . stealing. I stole baby clothes and food to help my sister until her food stamps kicked in. You see, my niece had a group of fathers: me, Cheyenne, some friends of ours and of course Yobanny, who was the man that wanted to be with my sister no matter what.

Even though I was stealing again, I still held down a job at Sears working in the bed and bath section. The money wasn't enough for what I was trying to do. I started recording again and decided to work, steal stuff, and re-sell it to make money to pay for some studio time. I was determined to put my first demo song together. I was only sixteen about to turn seventeen years old and I had written my very first song from the beginning to the end. I was tired of hearing my friends and family telling me what an incredible voice I had and how I could send shivers and goose bumps up their spine. I was determined to do something with my talent. I knew Cheyenne always wanted to be a singer as well, but he gave up. Another dream that went down the drain.

I remember using my father's old microphone and recording equipment that was in the house to record the rough draft. I used a beat from a song that already existed, so that I could have a rhythm to follow. I wrote the song in one day alone at the house. That night I called my father, sisters, and brother into the living room at my father's house and asked them to sit down and listen to something. They all sat down, anticipating what I was going to play them. At first they seemed a bit annoyed that I was bothering them, I could see it in their faces that they did not want to be there, wasting their time. I hit play . . . .

The shocked look on their faces was priceless. My father closed his eyes and smiled as he heard it and then would turn serious when he heard me hitting certain notes, as if he was singing it with me. They were all happy and excited for me and my father immediately said, "Give me a copy of that, Son. I have to find friends that have a studio where you can record a final copy and possibly re-do the beat to be your own." I looked at Cheyenne and even though he was happy for me, I saw a look of disappointment in his face. As if maybe he lost focus on his goal of being a singer a little too soon.

I finished up my first demo, "Can't Stand Being Played," the song I wrote and composed with a great producer my father introduced me to. This producer was able to re-create my own beat to the song so I owned not just the lyrics, but also the beat. What motivated me the most was when I met a woman who worked for Sony Records and she heard about the song I wrote through the producer. I wanted my brother Cheyenne and sister Yazmin to be my backup singers, so we could make it a family project. We went back to the studio lab and for once, my older brother and sisters were looking up to me. They had to listen to me tell them how I wanted them to sing. Here I was, 17-years-old, telling my big brother that I didn't like his voice and to 'do it again' until it was perfect. Cheyenne would get aggravated with me and punch the ceiling, but we had to perfect song. This was our "baby," so we had to get it right.

After months of working in the studio, going to school, playing sports and trying to make money on the side the "honest" way, we finally finished the song. Cheyenne, Yazmin, and I had a photo shoot booked for our promo CD to submit to Sony. I was trying to lose as much weight as possible, but it wasn't working, so I just gave up and told myself, there are a lot of fat singers out there, so I'll just be another one. About a month later Cheyenne and I went to a softball game at Rutgers's University in New Jersey where his girlfriend, Nikki, was playing. It was the first time in a long time that we hung out together. We took a walk to a creek and we sat together, looking at the water.

"You know," Cheyenne said, "ever since we were kids I always begged dad to listen to my songs . . . hear the music me and my friends made and sang when we had our music group. He never did, Kari. Never! He wanted me to just join the Marine Corps. That's all that mattered to him."

Tears began to fall from Cheyenne's eyes. I asked him why he was crying. When he looked at me with his eyes all red, I couldn't help but cry too.

"Because all I ever wanted was Dad to support me on my music and, look, he supports you. Why did you put me in that song?"

I told Cheyenne that we are a family and the group was a family business. I said, "It was Dad's idea to put you and Yazmin in the song. He supports us all on this one. When you were younger, Dad probably felt you weren't ready. But he knows you're ready now."

Cheyenne just looked down at the creek. He said, "No, Kari, it's not right."

"Cheyenne, we are going to get through this together," I said. "We have Sony Records on the back burner."

Trying to add humor, I continued, "Pretty soon you are going to be fighting all these girls off you when they hear your voice."

31

"Kari, the only girl I want left me years ago," my brother confided. "Lina was the best. She was my everything, Kari. Why am I with this girl, Nikki? Do I really love her? Am I just trying to fill a void?" His tears kept falling.

I told him that he's worrying about the past and that we have to move on to the present and future. That all the things he was upset about were old and that tomorrow is a new day. We sat together as Cheyenne continued to cry. I told him how much I loved him and admired the things he did. I admitted to him how much I wanted to be like him. I admitted how jealous I was as a kid of him because he was "All American", beautiful, strong, smart, sincere, and loved by everyone. I told him Nikki was a great girl for him and that Lina was just an "ex".

"I am no one and there is nothing I have to be admired," Cheyenne said.

For some odd reason, I noticed my brother growing closer to me, as if we were friends. It was weird because I remembered all our fights and arguments. Cheyenne would beat me until I was left for dead in the street, but the next day I would look at him and love him like nothing in the world. My mind started rambling on to funny times we had. Like the week prior we were playing Play Station in the living room, just me and him at our house. All of a sudden I saw someone in the corner of my eye in a white gown going up the stairs from the entrance to my dad's townhouse. I didn't want to acknowledge it because it was pretty creepy and I didn't know if I was just seeing things, so I focused more into the game. And then, Cheyenne paused the game and asked, "Kari, did you just see what I saw in the mirror?"

"Chayi, please don't tell me you saw the white lady!"

"Yep," he said, "with long white hair."

Oh my God! We both dropped the controllers and ran downstairs screaming like little girls. We told my father and he said that it was his mother's spirit. We didn't care who it was—it shouldn't have been there! We later laughed about it and named her, "The White Lady." Later that week, our good friend Kino ran into "The White Lady" while waiting for me and my sister, Yassina, to come to the house. He got so scared that he jumped off the second floor balcony to my dad's townhouse! He never came over alone again.

A couple weeks after our talk at the creek, my father and Cheyenne were fighting. Cheyenne wanted to go to pilot school, but my father kept yelling at him, telling him to stop looking across the street and that the grass is not greener on the other side.

"Suck it up and keep working regular jobs," Dad said.

The argument got so bad I had to get between the two so nobody would throw a punch. I could feel the anger, frustration and pain my big brother was feeling . . . pain he had bottled up inside himself. But I couldn't help him.

One night my sister Yassina and I were watching a movie about Selena, the Mexican singer who was murdered by her obsessive manager of her fan club. While we watched the movie, Dad was getting ready for a vacation he was going on with his girlfriend at the time, which was also my brother's boss. Nobody at Cheyenne's job knew my father and Cheyenne were related due to the "no family" policy. As Dad was getting ready for his vacation, he glanced over at the television and said, "That's the worst thing a parent has to do—having to bury his or her own child."

A couple days later I was supposed to go on a church trip for a week in Canada, but a girl named Jennifer asked me to the Junior Prom. I never intended on going to the prom because I didn't have a date and I wasn't ready to be turned down by girls in school. Jennifer asked me and I didn't know if I should go because we were a day away from the prom and I knew it would be impossible to find a tuxedo. I took a couple hours to think about it and talk to my best friend Rod. Finally, I decided, why not? Something inside told me not to go on the church trip to Canada, so I decided to follow my instincts. Little did I know that decision was given to me by God and made me a part of something that changed my life forever.

My Junior Prom was on a Friday, May 22, 1998. My mother, brother, sisters and friends were all at my house with me and my date taking pictures. It was great. My mother was so happy to see me in a tuxedo. Cheyenne and his girlfriend Nikki dropped us off at the prom.

"I'm happy you didn't go to the church trip, Kari," my brother said. "You only have a Junior Prom once bro, trust me."

The prom was a night I will never forget. As I was dancing with Jennifer I heard the DJ say, "Ladies and gents, this next song is your very truly one and only, Karim Ramos, in a hit single called 'Can't Stand Being Played.' Here we go!"

The beat kicked on and my heart dropped to the floor. I stood there wondering who the heck gave him my song because I didn't! Everyone kept coming up to me, congratulating me, and telling me how much they liked it. I went up to the only person who heard it before.

"Rod, was this you, bro?"

He just stared and smiled.

I grabbed him and asked, "When did you get the CD?"

"Cheyenne gave it to me . . . to play at the prom."

I put my arm around Rod and we stood there and just watched everyone dance to the song I recorded with my big brother and sister. What an amazing feeling.

On May 24, 1998, I was playing Play Station with three of my friends at my house, when I received a call from Cheyenne. Nikki's birthday was the night before and Cheyenne had stayed at his friend's house. When I picked up the phone I noticed there was something wrong with him. I didn't know what it was at the time. Cheyenne was calling me from his job at the airport.

"Hey, Kari."

"Chayi, what's up bro?"

"Nothing much, what are you doing?" The tone of his voice told me something was wrong.

"What's wrong?"

"Nothing," Cheyenne said. "I want you to know something, Kari, I never told you this, but I admire you and have always admired you."

"Why are you crying?" I asked, cutting him off.

I was listening to my super hero cry, so I began crying too.

"What is wrong, bro? We have our demo finished and all we have to do is our photo shoot next week and submit the package to Sony Records."

"Why?! Why did you put me on that song?!" he asked, painfully.

"'Cause we are family and this is a family business and we are talented and the world should hear us! Why are you crying? What's wrong, bro?"

"Nothing's wrong. Your whole life you wanted to be a singer and would run around the house singing into a brush, trying to make Dad see what you had. But Dad always wanted Yazmin to be the singer! He didn't want you! But look at how your hunger and strive worked! You kept singing and now he's paying for your studio time and trying to get you and your voice out there!"

"I understand, Chayi, but we are doing this now! You and me, bro! Forget about what Dad did and didn't do! We are here now and I need you!"

"Kari, just know that I admire you. You get whatever you want and you don't stop until you get it. I love you. Put Yazmin on the phone."

"Wait, Chayi, am I seeing you tonight?"

"I don't know."

In my mind, I wasn't thinking anything bad. He slept over his friend's house the night before, so I thought he was spending the night again.

"Well, I love you bro, and I hope to see you tonight," I said. "Remember you are my super hero."

I had no idea what was happening. I remember my heart was pounding. My ears were clogged after that conversation. I couldn't hear what any of my friends were saying to me because I couldn't understand what the message was that Cheyenne was really trying to tell me. I handed the phone to Yazmin and said, "It's Cheyenne and he doesn't sound right."

She grabbed the phone and I left her room and sat down on the living room sofa. My friends kept asking me what was wrong, but the knot in my stomach wouldn't let me speak. So I shrugged my shoulders and nodded my head from left to right, two times. Moments later, Yazmin came running out of her room and said, "Stay near the phone, I have to go to the airport!" She threw the phone to me and I asked her if everything was all right. She just ran outside and jumped in her car with my mother.

I went to the kitchen and sat down on the floor with a sculpture made out of steal that my father found in the garbage. I was rocking back and forth, replaying the phone conversation in my head that I just had with my brother. I had no idea what was happening. My mind was racing a hundred miles a minute. I couldn't say anything to my friends, so I left them alone and let them continue playing Play Station. I just sat there, waiting for someone to call on the phone like my sister said. A million questions came to mind. I couldn't imagine my brother—my super hero—doing anything to himself, in any harmful way. This is the man made of steel—the man that could handle anything—the man that had it all! No, I didn't know what to expect.

Then the phone rings.

"Yes?" I answered.

It was my brother's best friend, Dom.

"Kari?"

I was too choked up to answer.

"Karim?"

"Yes, what is going on with my brother?"

Dom's voice sounded sad and shocked as he answered, "Kari, wait a minute . . ."

"No! No! Dom, I'm not waiting! What happened to my big brother?! Where is Cheyenne? No! Don't freaking tell me! Don't you dare tell me what I think you're going to say! Don't Dom! Oh my God . . . what?!"

"Chayi hung himself. They don't know if he's alive."

Immediately after that sentence I couldn't hear anything Dom was saying. I felt like someone punched me in both ears at the same time and all you hear is a ringing echo. All I can remember from that point on was I threw the steel statue that was in my lap across the room. I screamed at the top of my lungs and said, "Nooooooo!" My friends came running over to me, asking what was wrong. I didn't answer them. I kept screaming and throwing everything in the living room around, crying. My mind had no thoughts, my heart had no beat, my bloody knuckles had no feeling in them. I ran out of the house, punching everything I saw. I ran downstairs and asked my friend if she could take to the airport. As I'm riding to Cheyenne's job, my mind is racing a million miles an hour. I can't think about anything but the last part Dom said, "They don't know if he's alive."

My body was numb.

As I pulled into the parking lot of my brother's job, I saw two officers wrapping his car with crime scene tape. My heart dropped even more. At this point everything around me did not exist. I felt like I was in the Twilight Zone. I got out of the car and ran up the stairs to his job—stairs that seemed to never end.

"Hey! Who are you? Where do you think you're going?" one of the police officers said, yelling.

I stopped, turned to the officer and said, "I'm looking for my brother."

"And who's that?" asked the officer.

"Cheyenne Ramos, sir."

The officer came up to the staircase, looked me in the eyes and said, "He's not here."

"Well, where is he?"

"The ambulance came and got him."

At this moment, I felt nothing. I grasped for air, one more time and asked, "Officer, do you know if he's alive?"

"No," the officer replied.

I said, "Wait . . . 'no, he's not alive' or 'no, you don't know'?"

He said, "No, he's not alive."

At that moment, I felt nothing. My legs got weak and my knees buckled out. I don't remember what happened after that, but I know I fell down the flight of stairs onto the ground. I don't remember exactly what happened but I felt someone pick me up off the ground and I started throwing punches and punched a police officer in the chest, not knowing who was manhandling me. Immediately I was slammed unto the police squad car and told by both officers to calm down or I was going to jail. When I regained consciousness and sight, I heard someone scream, "Karim!"

I heard the voice, but my eyes wouldn't let me focus. I took a second, closed my eyes real tight, then looked up at the top of the staircase where my brother's office was and I saw my sister Yassina standing there, crying. Yassina ran downstairs and hugged me. She cried a river as she hugged me tighter.

"I can't believe he did it! He did it, Kari! Why? Why? Why?"

As I held her and squeezed her, all I could say was, "Yassina, why did he do this? What happened? Oh my God! Where's Mom? Where's Mom?"

Yassina said she went to the hospital with Yazmin. I asked why, but Yassina's tears and screams wouldn't let her finish the sentence, so I repeated the question, "Yassina, why did Mom go to the hospital?"

"Because Yazmin hyperventilated and passed out."

At this moment, so much has happened to me that I felt like running upstairs and breaking down the door to do exactly what my big brother did. The questions ran through my mind once again: How? Why me? How? How? How? Meanwhile, all this has happened and my father was still on vacation with his girlfriend, who was my brother's boss, in Florida. If my father only knew he was going to be putting his foot in his mouth by having to do exactly what he said was the worst thing a parent can do when watching the movie about Selena.

Yassina and I drove to the hospital to see Yazmin and my mother. I can't imagine what was running through my mother's mind and heart when she arrived at the airport before me and saw her first baby boy being carried on a stretcher. Upon our arrival we see Mom standing outside smoking a cigarette, crying on the phone to someone. I yelled, "Mami!" She looked over her shoulder and I ran as fast as I could while tears were crawling down my face. As my mother squeezed me and cried, the only thing that ran through my mind was how can somebody as sweet and loving, as my mother, have to face this? Cheyenne committed suicide and didn't even consider his family's thoughts, feelings and emotions.

Yassina ran to Mom and me and hugged both of us. Here we are—the three of us—just hugging and crying in a circle outside the very hospital my brother was laying in for committing suicide. And my sister Yazmin was laying in, drugged up for nearly having a heart attack. In Spanish, my mother just kept saying, "My baby boy did it! Why? Why did he abandon me and do this sin?" All I could do was squeeze her and say, "Mom, we are all that's left. We have to be strong and pray to God." Yassina continued to cry a river.

We walked in the hospital to check on Yazmin. She was okay, just sleeping when we got there. The doctor gave her sleeping meds. Immediately we were all trying to call friends and family to give the news. Yassina called Cheyenne's first love, Lina, and had to explain to her that Cheyenne is gone. My mother called all the relatives. Nobody could get in contact with my father because he was on the plane returning back to Newark from his vacation in Florida with his girlfriend.

I called my friends Rod, Kino and John. We were the last three guys that spent Cheyenne's last months with him. I looked at those guys like brothers and Cheyenne knew that. When I called them, they all thought I was joking because this was not a "Cheyenne move." We all looked up to Cheyenne. The man that was an altar boy, model, singer, actor and one of the best looking guys that even dated his own substitute teacher in school! It was a nightmare for all of us. We all didn't think it was real. My friends rushed to the hospital. Dom was there and so were both of my sister's friends to help show support.

I explained to Mom that Cheyenne called all of us to basically say his good-byes. Yassina said she never got a call. We later found out he didn't call Yassina because at the time he committed suicide Yassina was working at a restaurant in the airport and Cheyenne probably knew she would rush there to stop him. My mother said she was standing right outside the office and could see her son's body lying on the floor, right next to where he hung himself. The cops stopped her and wouldn't let her pass. My mother screamed, with her broken English, "That's my son! That's my baby boy! Please let me see my baby boy!" The officers continued to push my mother back forbidding her entrance. "Let me feel my son one last time, please!" That's when Yazmin hyperventilated and passed out.

The same day Cheyenne committed suicide my father's flight was arriving to Newark from his vacation in Florida. Now you have to remember, my father was traveling with his girlfriend who was Cheyenne's supervisor. You have to also remember that nobody knew that Cheyenne and Dad were related. They all thought it was just a coincidence. As my father and his girlfriend step off the plane, a police officer that knew my father approached him. "Hey, did you hear what happened today?"

"No, what happened?" my father asked.

The officer said, "Yeah, some Ramos kid committed suicide today—about an hour ago." He had no idea that the "Ramos Kid" was his friend's son!

My father dropped to his knees in the airport and cried.

I can just imagine what my father was feeling at this time, as he listened to the officers talk about "this Ramos kid" that hung himself in the ladies restroom in his office about an hour or two before their flight landed. My father and his girlfriend went straight to the site where Cheyenne committed suicide. I'm sure my father's heart and mind were racing at this moment. They arrived and spoke with the investigators. Being that my father is a federal agent, the officers had no idea it was his son, so they showed my father the pictures of Cheyenne's body of how they found him. I don't think I'd be able to control my composure like my father did. Just imagine, some cop showing you pictures of how they found your son's body when he committed suicide.

We all met up with my father at the hospital. Tears kept falling from all our eyes. My father hugged my mother and I stood there watching them cry. It was like they felt they had failed as parents and did not want us to know. We decided we were going to the house to have a gathering for our friends and family. At the house it was so quiet you could hear a needle hit the floor. There were about 30 people in a two-bedroom townhouse. Here we were, all in shock, not knowing what to say to each other.

I went outside to the balcony with my father and we just sat there looking at the stars together—just him and me. I didn't have any words to tell my father. I just stood there and I could see his mind was racing a million miles per minute. He looked at me and said, "When I got to, the police officers showed me pictures of Cheyenne's body."

"How did my brother look?"

Dad said, "Kari, just remember your brother when he was alive." Tears rolled down his face and he hugged me again.

Continuing, he said, "Karim, you are the man of the house now. You have no choice but to lead the family and be that backbone for your mother and sisters. Tomorrow when you wake up, you will no longer be a child; you will no longer be able to mess around with your friends. Your mother and sisters need you. I hope you are ready and want the responsibility. You have to do this for the family, and most importantly, your brother."

I knew at that moment that I was going from a boy to a man overnight and my thoughts and actions were going to have to change. My father wanted him buried within a day. No obituary was created for him. We had the wake one day, and then the next day was the burial. The day of the funeral, we all went up to Cheyenne's open casket at the same time. I was holding on to my mother and my father was holding on to my sisters.

The moment you could see Cheyenne's face, my mother started to cry and scream. She laid her head in my chest and I held her fragile body tight. I couldn't show any emotion because I was afraid that my tears and true feelings would make things worse. So I held my sisters and mother while they cried. My father and I just shed a tear or two, trying to remain calm and control the situation. After my mother and sisters found their seats, they put down their belongings and began receiving hugs and kisses for their loss.

I found my free moment to approach Cheyenne's casket alone. I walked up and all I could see was the top of his face. I began examining his features. His eyes were puffy; his neck, swollen; the black and blue colors were hidden behind the cheap make-up that the funeral home used. At this moment my heart wasn't working, so my feelings were kept in. I put one hand on his hand that was holding my mother's rosary. I caressed his head with my other hand. I leaned over and gave him a kiss on the forehead. I whispered in his ear, "Please, wake up. Chayi, come on, bro, wake up. Come on, man, stop playing. Wake up, bro."

Cheyenne just laid there stiff and cold as ice. I realized he wasn't getting up. I leaned back over to him and I said, "Chayi, I can bring you back to life. They didn't really try, bro. I can do it." For some reason I really thought I could bring him back, but then reality hit me and I realized my brother was gone . . . that Cheyenne was not coming back.

I squeezed his hand tighter.

As I kissed his forehead again, I realized my teardrop landed on his face and right at that moment, when I saw he didn't even flinch I began crying harder and harder. I let go and ran out of the funeral home as fast as I could. I got outside and began walking fast and crying as I repeated to myself that I could not believe Chayi is dead. Not knowing where I was going, I just kept walking out of anger, disappointment and confusion. All of a sudden, I heard voices. "Karim, wait! Come here!" It was my friends, Rod, Kino and John. They grabbed me and started hugging me.

Here I was in a circle of my closest friends, just crying in the middle of the street as they kept repeating that I was their brother and that I might have lost one brother, but gained three more. From that moment on, I knew they were the only brothers I had left.

Back at the funeral, my mother and father were fighting about my father allowing his ex-girlfriend into the funeral home. I walked in and I saw my mother yelling at my father and his ex-girlfriend for the lack of respect towards his dead son. My mother felt like his ex-girlfriend was one of the reasons they got divorced. My father was seeing this woman for 10 years behind my mother's back! I was crushed to see my mother screaming like this at her son's funeral.

My father's ex-girlfriend came in, paid her respects and I could hear my mother screaming, "Don't you dare touch my son!" Moments later, after everything calmed down, she left and my father sat next to his girlfriend, at the time. My father's bosses came with about 100 other law enforcement officers to pay their respects. My father left with his supervisor to hand in his two guns. When a family member dies, I guess it's a protocol to confiscate the weapons to prevent accidents or any danger that the officer can do to himself or his family. My guidance counselor, Anne D'Nicola, asked the principal that there be a moment of silence for Cheyenne throughout the school. The principal also granted permission to students that wanted to leave to pay their respects to Cheyenne. The faces of friends, teachers and people I didn't even know amazed me.

My brother was buried in a military cemetery and at the funeral hall Marine soldiers that were standing next to Cheyenne's casket greeted us. This was our last chance to see our brother and son . . . the last time to see and touch Cheyenne physically. I walked up to his casket and placed a photo of him, and me when we were kids, in his pocket. I leaned over to him and, in his ear, I said, "I love you, bro. Take this picture of us—that's how I will remember you. I will keep my copy forever." Then I kissed him on his forehead and then walked to my seat.

There were about 250 people at the burial ceremony. Everyone that knew Cheyenne, from just being his family or a friend, or an ex-girlfriend, to complete strangers, were there for the family. I remember it was so quiet and the priest said, "Let's take a moment of silence for Cheyenne Jonathan Ramos." At this time I just looked around and saw all these caring, sad faces. I closed my eyes, looked up to the ceiling and started singing Boyz II Men's song "It's So Hard to Say Goodbye to Yesterday." I didn't realize that I was singing it! My mind went into a separate room from my voice. I started singing it and in the middle of singing it, my sister Yazmin grabbed my side and started singing along with me. When I opened my eyes, I realized everyone in the room was singing the words. Two hundred fifty people in a small room were all singing, "It's So Hard to Say Goodbye to Yesterday."

It was amazing! I couldn't believe the energy in that room. At first people thought someone brought a radio to the funeral and said to themselves that was so disrespectful. Then other people swore they heard two voices coming out of my mouth and that Cheyenne was in me singing! I don't know what happened or how I started singing but I'm glad I did and it was an honor to see everyone get involved and show his or her love to my brother on this very sad occasion.

After Cheyenne was buried, we all left to Nikki's house for a reception. Back at home we all had to face reality and deal with all the situations we had with Cheyenne's death. Well, it turned out Cheyenne left letters for all of us saying his goodbyes. An officer found those letters at the crime scene and gave them to my father. Everyone's letter pretty much said the same thing: "I love you, please forgive me and keep your head up."

I decided I wanted you all to see my letter from my brother before he committed suicide.

(Cheyenne's goodbye letter hand written on next page)

I snuck this picture into Cheyenne's pocket at his funeral.

Me & Cheyenne (The Last Time)

Karim   5-24-98   10

I'm SORRY BRO! PLEASE
FORGIVE ME. I WANT YOU TO
KNOW THAT I LOVE YOU WITH
ALL MY HEART. I'M SORRY I'M
NOT THE PERFECT BROTHER.
BUT I LOVE YOU AND I'M VERY
PROUD OF YOU MORE THAN
YOU THINK I KNOW YOU WILL
SUCCEED IN LIFE. KEEP YOUR
HEAD UP. I LOVE YOU

LOVE ALWAY
YOUR BIG BROTHI
Chay!

CHAPTER 4

The Road to Risk

"I've realized you are as successful as you want to be. Nothing stands in your way, but a little thing called DOUBT. . . . "Don't doubt yourself." Karim Ramos

Cheyenne's death was a rude awakening. You would imagine that the family would grow closer. Well, we did, but that was a temporary thing. So many questions were left up in the air that weren't answered. When Cheyenne died, his car was left at the airport in front of his job. My father allowed Amber to clean out Cheyenne's desk at work, since she was his boss, leaving not a trace. She was allowed to clean out his car too! I went to his car to see if he left clues. Maybe something happened to him that we did not know about. But all that was left were a set of 20 lb. dumbbells.

Cheyenne always had life insurance and would always leave 100 percent of it to my mother, no matter where he went. Well, according to Cheyenne's supervisor, Cheyenne had no life insurance. About a week later, my mother was called by another business, a part-time job Cheyenne held, to sign the life insurance he left behind for her. She had to go to the business with his death certificate and sign documents. I stayed by her side and watched her sign above the dotted line. Suddenly, I noticed her hand stopped signing. She was crying. I grabbed her hand and said, "Mommy, please just sign it so we can leave!"

"I lost my baby boy and all my son's life is worth to this company is $10,000?"

Back in school, my senior year began. I noticed a lot of change in the attitudes of my teachers towards me. I confronted my guidance counselor, Mrs. D, who I consider a very special friend. She was with me throughout my years at John F. Kennedy High School and most important, when I lost Cheyenne. I asked her if it was just me or were people acting a little different, treating me with more sensitivity. She said that they probably were showing me their sorrow because of what I went through. I didn't know how to take it and I told her I didn't like that.

Mrs. D always knew what to say to her student to help them out. I remember the day I sat in Mrs. Ds office and asked her "Mrs. D, what's my purpose? . . . Why am I here? . . . Will I succeed in life or be another failure?" There goes those infamous questions: "Why? Why? Why?"

Mrs. D looked at me straight in my eyes, grabbed both of my hands and said, "Karim you are a wonderful, giving person, with so much ahead of you. You have so many talents and gifts, but your biggest gift is your heart. You make people feel good."

She continued, "Karim if there is one thing I am certain, whether you go to a four-year college or not, you are one of the very few people I can say that will go far in life just because of your heart and personality. I do not worry about you at all."

After that conversation I ended up helping students that were having personal problems with family, drugs, personnel issues, or even students that just needed an ear to listen. It was a great feeling that led me to receiving a scholarship check for $380 from psychology originations for helping students. It was an accomplishment that had me lost for words. When the tragic incident happened at Columbine High School, my psychology teacher wanted the students to write letters expressing our sincere apologies for their losses. I wrote the following poem:

Colorado Went Through
By: Karim Ramos

As I sit in class
All I think about is Colorado
A school with such a bad memory
I pray it don't follow
A school with different places
A school now with tears down their faces
A school whose life was once fine
A school whose life is now destroyed in such short time
Why oh why
Would someone have to go through this
Why oh why
Should someone's life feel ludicrous
The looks on their faces
The feelings inside
The beautiful hearts that had to hide
The feeling in your mind
That you don't know if you're going to live or die
The sounds of yelling
The sounds of screaming
The sounds of bodies dropping
That sounds unbelieving
What those beloved families who lost
Their loved one must have been feeling
I'll never understand
But I imagine its UN-healing
The world isn't going to end
By Mother Nature's time
But by the gun that a person holds
In your face
In your eyes
What is the world coming to

What's there to say or do
But for the families who have lost
One or two
Please know my love and blessings are
With you
For those that can't handle anger in a positive way
Don't take a persons future or dreams and make it their last day
Be strong and live long
Is all we can do
I really pray that no one else
Has to go through what
Colorado went through . . .

It turned out that poem was bigger than I thought. Mrs. D and my psychology teacher sent a copy of it to our president, at the time; Bill Clinton's office and I received a "thank-you" letter from him. The poem was published in my school paper, and I was asked to read it to my fellow students over the announcement speaker system that ran throughout the school.

At this time my father and I were living together but I felt like I was a burden. I wasn't comfortable with the idea of having his wife—the woman he left my mother for—living with us. My father decided to surprise my sisters and me one day and brought us to an old building in a small shopping center. We walked inside and it was an old abandoned café. My father asked us, "What do you think?"

My sisters and I had no idea what he meant and stood there looking puzzled.

"Welcome to Don Chayi's!" Dad said. "Kids, I am buying this place for you guys, so we can open up a restaurant and name it after your brother, Cheyenne."

We were all shocked. We asked my father where he got the money and how are we going to do this. Dad said it was a gift from him to us—that he borrowed the money from some friends. Every day after school my friends and I would go to the restaurant to help out. Little by little we finished and then had a family business. Although she didn't want to be negative, my mother admitted that she thought my father got the money from Cheyenne's life insurance at the place where he committed suicide. We will never know the truth, but I told my mother not to worry about it—that this was something Cheyenne would want us to do.

We were the only restaurant in our area that sold both Puerto Rican and Cuban food and delivered to so many offices and stores and residents. When I graduated high school my life was devoted to the restaurant. The entire family worked from 7 a.m. till 11:30 p.m., seven days a week. My father worked his regular 9 to 5 job, and then came to the restaurant. He always told me one of the important things you need to run a successful business is to have good customer service. So if our grills were off and we were closed, mopping the floors and someone came to our door to see if we were open, my father would unlock the door and welcome them in. We would all have to turn everything on and start cooking again.

Ninety percent of our business was deliveries. Our marketing concept was the cheapest out there—word of mouth and flyers. We'd come into the restaurant at 7 a.m. and there were literally piles of faxed orders. When you work hard and devote your time and efforts to something in hopes that you will see money, you tend to lose motivation after a while. My mother, sisters and I worked so hard but never saw a penny. My father would give us 20 bucks for gas—and that was that. So we ended up hating our business. I know my father was paying people back for funds borrowed, but my sisters lost focus of the potential and decided they wanted out and wanted to move to back to Florida. At this point Yassina's daughter Thalia (my god daughter) was getting older and she needed to spend as much time with her and husband Yobanny, so I couldn't help but understand her. It crushed my father that all this hard work and time he put in came to an end. I ask my father if I could run it alone and dad said, "No it's too difficult." So he sold the business. So much animosity and anger developed in all of us since we worked so hard—for nothing.

Next, I found myself working as a waiter at a Mexican restaurant in New Jersey and stayed to live with my father, while my mother and sisters moved back to Ocala, Florida. I noticed my relationship with Dad was getting worse and worse the day I asked him to pay for my college. He immediately denied that request and told me that if I want to go to college I should pay for it myself. After that day our relationship started changing. I noticed we disagreed so much. It was like the relationship Cheyenne and Dad had before Cheyenne died. So I decided to move back to Ocala, with the rest of my family.

Back in Ocala? How is that possible? Why? Why did I feel like I was taking 10 steps backwards? Going back to my hometown, back to horse farms, I didn't get it. Here I was staying at my mother's house, living with my mother and sisters Yazmin and Yassina, my goddaughter Thalia, and my sister's husband Yobanny—all of us under the same roof.

Here I am, a twenty year old, feeling like I failed at my music opportunity when Cheyenne died. So even though my body was in Florida, my heart was in New Jersey—and New York. My mother saw me as a zombie in neutral. So I got a job as a trainer at the YMCA. I was a trainer and found myself trying to learn everything I could to better myself. When the bosses at the YMCA saw my personal skills with members and realized I was a tool they could utilize, they sent me to a personal training five-day course. I learned personal training and nutrition—all on the company's account. I came back with more knowledge to help more people who were lost and confused with nutrition, health, and their physical abilities. I was determined to change my lifestyle, bad eating habits, and get into shape. I didn't want to be in Ocala because I felt I was destined to be in the city. I felt like I was bigger then Ocala, not out of cockiness but bigger in the sense of finding my way to the entertainment industry. But how? I'm in Ocala, Florida and I want to get to the Big Apple.

I had a great time teaching fitness, I averaged about 15 private sessions a week, taught 15-minute abs classes, and I ended up becoming a boot camp drill instructor, training 30 individuals who all lacked either motivation, discipline or fitness abilities, or wanted to lose weight. I was not in my best shape but at that time I thought I was in the best shape I could be. In almost a year, I went from 262lbs. to 215lbs. It wasn't easy but I was determined to be like my brother Cheyenne.

One day I was training this lady who was trying to lose 30 lbs. in a month for her wedding. I never told her it was impossible. I trained her and got her to her goal weight in exactly 35 days. I remember looking in her eyes and telling her, "I didn't lose the thirty pounds, you did! You did it all on your own 'cause you didn't give up. You saw the opportunity and you took it!"

I went home that day and told my mother that I had to go back to New Jersey. My mother looked at me like I was crazy.

"Son, where are you going to stay? Your father is remarried and you have no other family there."

As worried as my mother was I told her I completely understand her being nervous and hesitant about supporting this decision. I told her, "Mom, I will be fine, I promise. I can't keep living my life with my mind in Florida and my heart in NYC. I feel like I was put here to change the world with my music. I feel like I need to work in the city, in the entertainment business. I want to feel important and feel like I'm a part of the city that doesn't sleep. We all dream of working in the Big Apple, but only some of us can actually do it."

My mother asked me when was I planning to make this move.

I said, "Tonight, Mom."

I could see it in her eyes that she thought I was nuts, but the look in my eyes said I was determined and did not want to do anything but move to either New Jersey or New York City. I had a goal and I needed to fulfill it before it was too late. I didn't want to be another person that regrets their life 10 years from now just because I was afraid to take a chance. I wasn't afraid to fall flat on my face. You can't be afraid to take a risk. The most successful people in this world like Oprah Winfrey, Donald Trump, or even Russell Simmons, all at on point risked all they had, and maybe even more, to get where they are today. I've heard an old saying that goes, "If you want to win big, then you have to risk big." I was risking everything.

That night I grabbed everything I owned which was a pair of sneakers, some clothes, my high school diploma and some pictures of my family. Then I jumped into my mother's 1991 Oldsmobile. This car was so old and beat up that the only heat I got was from the engine. Only one window worked up and down. I didn't look at it like a piece of junk; I looked at it like a good car that took me from point A to point B. It was motivation because I know everything is only as temporary as we make it.

Here I was driving on the highway heading back to New Jersey with nothing to my name but a couple shirts, two pairs of jeans, a jacket, and a pair of sneakers. With just barely enough money in my wallet to pay for gas and tolls, I had no idea what I was thinking. The only thing that kept coming into my mind was that I had to make this move now or I never would. I drove a straight 16 hours from Ocala, FL to Woodbridge, NJ. Making a pit stop before beginning a journey to the unknown, I stood in front of Cheyenne's grave. In the dark, I sat in the dirt and spoke to the tombstone as if he were right in front of me. I told Cheyenne that I had no idea how I was going to make it to the music industry but I felt destined to do it. I was scared to death and knew that if I failed, I wasn't going to fail without a fight.

I cried and cried. I felt so alone. I felt like I was being punished for something I was unaware of. I fell asleep on the ground by Cheyenne's grave for about an hour.

Then I proceeded to Woodbridge for the beginning of my new life. I had no idea where to go, so I went to the park and fell asleep in my car and prayed that night that God just protect me and give me guidance. The next day I went to see my father. I had the keys to get in so I just let myself in so I could get some food before I began the job searching. I got to the house and his new wife, Sandy, was in the kitchen. I had no idea she was home.

"Hey Kari, what are you doing inside my house?" I was so startled that Sandy would talk to me like that, especially in the house I spent all of my middle and high school years in—with my family! I looked at her and said, "Sorry, Dad gave me a copy of the house key and told me if I ever needed anything like food or a place to stay that I was more then welcome."

"You should knock," she said.

"Next time I will! Sorry." I grabbed a banana and left to my job search.

That same night I came back to my father's house. As I was walking up the staircase to see Dad, I noticed some new doorknobs in their packages sitting there. I didn't give them any mind. I went up to Dad and gave him a big hug and kiss. He asked me why was I back and wanted to know what I was planning to do with myself. I simply told him I was job-hunting at the moment. We sat there and talked for maybe 20 minutes. I felt so uncomfortable about being there, like I was being watched or something after what happed early that morning. My father asked me where I was going to sleep. I knew Sandy's daughter was sleeping in the room that used to belong to me, so just to make it seem like I didn't need that from him I said, "At my friend Rod's house." After I left his house, I went right back to the park to sleep again. I only had a couple dollars, so I couldn't afford a place to live or even a hotel. I didn't want to contact my best friend Rod or any of my other friends because I was embarrassed to be living out of my car with no money.

The following day I went back to my fathers to get another banana and a drink. The doors were changed with different lock. My heart dropped. I was crushed. I felt betrayed by the same man I used to look up to. I went on two interviews and then back to my father's to ask for a copy of the keys to the door because he promised me the house will always be mine too, and that I was always welcome there no matter whom he married. So I go to his house, the door was unlocked and he and Sandy were lying on the couch watching TV.

"Hey, Dad. Hey, Sandy. How's everything?"

My father was in a good mood and said, "Hey, Son, everything is good."

I didn't want to sit down because I was nervous and scared at the same time. I wanted to know why the locks were changed, so I asked him, "Papi, what happened to the doors? You changed the locks."

"Yea, Son . . . Sandy and I agreed that too many people had copies to the key to get in the house, so we decided to change them."

"Where is my copy?"

Dad looked at me, as he was still sitting on the couch, and I was standing at the door and said, "Well, Son, we don't think you need a copy either . . . sorry."

My voice got louder as I said, "Wait a minute . . . you are locking me out of the house?"

I noticed the smirk on Sandy's face as if to say, "Hah! I told you so."

I couldn't help but to scream anything that came to my mind at this point, so I yelled, "You have to be freaking kidding me! You throw your only son on the street, with no food . . . for this freaking woman?!"

My father tried standing up, like he was going to punch me again. I looked at him and said, "Dad, don't stand up or we will definitely swing out!"

He looked at me and knew, for once in our lives, I was standing up to him. I said, "Dad, you are wrong and you know it. You crushed me."

Continuing, I added, "Don't worry, Dad, I will see myself out." And I left.

That night I went back to my apartment—the park.

I couldn't really talk to my mother or friends over the phone because my cell phone was pre-paid and I had to save my minutes for possible job calls. I eventually had to use the pay phone from a hotel as my home number on applications for jobs. I finally landed a job as a waiter at TGI Fridays. I tried to make the best of it and started singing Happy Birthday songs in an R&B style. Before you knew it people were coming up to the host and requesting me as their waiter so I could sing "Happy Birthday" for them.

One day, a man with three of his friends overheard me singing and asked me to sing another song to them, so I did. Then a bald guy with a big necklace asked me to sing another song, so I did. Then another guy came up to me and asked where I was from. I said I was born in Puerto Rico but I live in Woodbridge. The guys asked me if I knew who the guy with the bald head and chains was. I said, "No."

They all looked at me like I was idiot. One of them said, "Yo, man, that's Damon Dash . . . are you serious, my dude?"

I looked at the man again, as another guy said, "Like, Roc-A-Fella Records . . . Damon Dash!"

I immediately cut them off and told him I knew who he was, but really thought he was just a look alike. I ended up singing one more song then they gave me a business card to call someone that following Monday. That night someone went into my locker and stole the business card, so I was never able to contact him. An opportunity missed, but it didn't stop me. I knew deep down inside when a door closes another door opens.

Within' two weeks of being back in New Jersey I ended up working four jobs. My schedule went like this:

* Personal training at a fitness center, 7 to 10 a.m.
* A waiter at a restaurant, 10:30 a.m. to 8 p.m.
* Singing R&B for a local DJ company, 9 to 11:30 p.m.
* Night security at dance clubs, bars and strip-clubs midnight to 4 a.m.

Then, I'd come back to the park to sleep, or just sit there talking to Cheyenne's spirit or God. I'd fall asleep around 5a.m. and get back up at 6:30a.m. Then do it all over again.

There were so many nights I wished I had the courage my brother had to pull the trigger, or hang myself. I had nobody! I couldn't talk to my friends and I couldn't console in my family, they would all panic if they knew I was living out of my mom's old Oldsmobile. But I was determined. I saw my goal. I had faith. And most of all I just believed in myself.

At this point I forgot what it felt like to have a warm cooked meal in my stomach. I forgot what it was like to have a nice warm shower. Instead I was paying a manager at a nearby hotel 10 bucks to let me shower real fast in a vacant room before I started my day. Stealing food from my waiter job started making me feel guiltier and guiltier even though it was just breadsticks and honey mustard. I was drinking one Snapple bottle a day as my breakfast, lunch, and dinner. Seeing other people happy was beginning to make me envious and jealous. Seeing fathers with their sons in the park walking and talking brought tears to my heart because I never had that with my father.

I related my lifestyle to rap music like Tupac's "Changes" or Biggie Small's "Sky's the Limit" or Jay Z's "Can't Knock the Hustle." My sleeping on the park bench days ended when I was able to afford a basement in an old lady's house. My park bench bed soon enough turned into a coffee table in an old basement. It had an old shower as well. I slept on the coffee table covered in my clothes to keep me warm with a little humidifier by face so I wouldn't breathe in the dust. I wore flip-flops after I took a shower so I wouldn't get my feet dirty again. But to me, it all felt like home. It was mine and I was paying $400 a month.

One day I remember I temporarily lost my mind and my true emotions came out. I was sitting on the coffee table not being able to sleep due to the noises of mice. For the first time in a long time I felt scared. I was afraid that I had failed in life. I was afraid of not being able to continue to live; I felt that should have been me in that coffin instead of my brother. With tears in my heart and eyes I screamed out loud, "What am I doing, God?! Why am I still here, working four jobs that will get me nowhere? Please, God, help me! Your lost son is seeking guidance! I thank you for my life and my family and friends, but I need a sign, God! Something to help me stay focused! I'm losing my faith. All this hard work I'm doing—for what?! To come to a dirty basement?! To live out of my car?! To not be able to tell my family and friends the truth, instead I would lie and say that I'm okay and fine?! Why?! How?! Why me?!"

Then softly, I said, "God, I am sorry for the anger and negative feeling. Please, All Mighty God, please help me put these broken pieces I made to my life back together. God, please be the driver to my bus while I am just the passenger. Without you, I am nothing."

I closed my eyes and slept that night, relieved, like a baby.

The very next day I was training with my regular client Katie, a lady who needed to build her muscles in her lower back. I trained with Katie for about four months. At the end of our session one day Katie asked me what my goals in life were. I said, "Well, I want to either be an entertainer, or write lyrics for artists that can change the world with their voices and music. If I couldn't do that I wanted to just work in the entertainment business and own my own business." She looked at me and asked, "Would you like to intern for me? I think it will help you accomplish some of those goals."

"Doing what?"

"Karim," Katie said, "I'm the VP of Retail Development and Graphic Designing for Baby Phat and Phat Farm."

"Wait a minute," I said. "You work for Mr. and Mrs. Simmons?"

"Yes," she said. "I think you're perfect for the job. It only pays 10 bucks a day as an intern, but you never know, maybe you'll get your chance to sing to Russell."

"But, why me?"

"Karim, you have a big heart, but you're so focused, and hustle hard. I've never heard you complain about your jobs or anything. You'd definitely appreciate this and I want to help you. Russell will love you, trust me."

"I would be honored to work for you, Katie. I am totally lost for words right now, please forgive me."

That night I went home and sat back on top of the coffee table, and for the first time in a long time I cried to God with appreciative, happy, and peaceful tears. I cried myself to sleep because He answered my prayers. I felt a shift in my universe, even though it was an internship, and only 10 dollars a day, I saw it as a career opportunity and a blessing.

"Thank you, God. Thank you, Cheyenne." My life was changing.

CHAPTER 5

A "PHAT" Prayer Was Answered

"From Horse Farms to Phat Farms." Karim Ramos

"One round trip ticket to New York City, please."

Here I was asking for my train ticket to the beginning of my new internship! The night before I was so nervous I barely slept. My coffee table bed felt like a down comforter king size bed. The Snapple bottle I drank in the morning for breakfast was like steak and eggs to my stomach, the cold shower in my flip flops felt like a spa. Nothing could bother me. I was too excited and thankful for my internship! That morning everything felt like I was in a five-star hotel. I knew one day I'd know what that really felt like, so I just kept pushing myself till I got there. I remember the feelings like it was yesterday.

What outfit to wear to my internship? You see Phat Farm is an "Urban" brand so I didn't want to go too over dressed. But I remember my father always telling me, "When you go to a job for the first time, always wear a suit because you never know what the bosses will expect you to wear." Dad also always used to say, "Your first impression is your last." So I wore my black dress pants and black shoes with my burgundy button up shirt and black and burgundy tie.

As I'm riding the train to my big first day I start regretting my dad's advice to "dress to impress." I didn't think it was a good idea to an urban branded company. Oh well . . . it was too late and I couldn't change on the train, so I just thought of all the positive things happening at that very moment. I couldn't believe I was on my way to New York City to work for Russell Simmons, Kimora Lee Simmons, and the Reverend Run from RUN DMC!!!

I told myself that I could get used to this commute, driving to the train station, hopping on a train with hundreds of business people from Wall Street to interns that were all working in the Big Apple. When I walked out of Penn Station I can remember the feeling and emotion that took over me that very moment. I mean here I was living my dream. The skyscrapers, the traffic, the bright lights, the billboards, the smell of food, the obnoxious New Yorkers rushing and pushing in every direction like they were running a marathon. But I loved it. I felt like I just didn't want it to end, so I thanked God.

I arrived to Phat Fashions on Seventh Avenue. As I stood in the front of the building, I took in every moment I could. I was struck by an all black Yukon Denali that pulled up. I see a man in a gray hooded zip-up sweat suit, a black Phat Farm hat, and black and white Phat Classic sneakers. It looked like this guy was just coming out of a photo shoot 'cause his clothes looked so fresh and new. "Mr. Simmons, have a nice day," the security man said.

I choked up! There he was—Russell Simmons, the godfather of hip hop, the founder of Def Jam Records, the man I used to always see at the end of Def Comedy Jam that always said his signature statement: "Thank you for coming, God bless and good night."

And there I was like an idiot, watching him go upstairs. He didn't notice my stupid facial expression. I went inside the building and told the security guard I was there to see Katie at Phat Farm. After showing my I.D., they let me in and I proceeded to the Phat Fashions Corporate office. I walked into the front reception and asked for Katie. The receptionist paged her and then Katie came out about five minutes later. Katie saw me, gave me a hug and said, "Welcome to Phat Fashions!"

So that day I was walked around being introduced to the president of Phat Fashions, Phat Farm staff, Baby Phat staff, and Rush Communications staff. It was an empire of multi-companies that Russell and his wife Kimora had. I remember walking by an office that that had two guys and a lady. They were playing hip hop music loud and just on the phones talking about different up-coming videos and associating Phat Farm in the videos.

I asked Katie, "Whose office is this?"

Kate said, "That's the marketing, public relations, and product placement office for Phat Farm."

I was like, "Now this is a place I see myself working in!"

"Karim, let me introduce you to the boss man," Katie said. We walked to his office that was right next to Katie's office. "Russell, this is my intern Karim Ramos."

"What up, Niggy? Good to have you with us."

"Thanks, Russell, my pleasure."

"Yo, why are you dressed in church clothes? This isn't that kind of company man. People are going to look at you like you crazy. Go see Myorr and tell him to get you some jeans and tees."

Continuing, he added, "Oh, and Karem, don't ever wear those shoes in here again."

"No problem Russ, I'll throw them out!" I didn't even care he called me "Karem."

Katie looked at me and said, "Yeah, I forgot to tell you the dress code here is relaxed. Let me take you to the marketing and PR department and introduce you to Myorr and Kevin."

We got to the room and Katie introduced us. "Myorr, this is Karim, my intern."

"What's up man? Working with Katie, huh? That's cool. She's a good person."

"This is Kev. Yo, Kev, this is Katie's intern Karim."

"Yoooo Niggy! What's up with your outfit? You going to the prom? Come on man what's up with the shoes? Are those Aldo's?" Kevin laughed.

Russell could hear Kevin's loud mouth, so he ran to the marketing office and said, "I know! Right Kev? Yo, get this niggy some fly outfits, please, we can't have him coming here like this no more." Russell laughed too.

Myorr said, "Welcome to Phat Farm. All we do is work and diss each other. You'll get used to it."

Back in the retail development and graphic designing department it was just Katie and I. I basically helped her design CADS and images for both Phat Farm and Baby Phat. To give you an example, Katie designed the floor layouts for major department stores that sold Phat Farm or Baby Phat. Katie's main job was to keep updating the floor layouts in major department stores like Macy's or Nordstrom's across the world so that customers will continue shopping the two brands.

I went home that night with five bags of Phat Farm clothing including two pairs of sneakers, two pairs of jeans, and four shirts! I couldn't believe my eyes. The feeling inside me felt like I was a millionaire, and in actuality, it was only a couple outfits. But when you have nothing and someone gives you something, no matter how big or small it is, you appreciate it with all your heart and soul.

That weekend I took home the clothes Myorr gave me and did my own photo shoot. I called my friend and asked him to meet me at a waterfront with his camera to take pictures of me modeling these outfits, so that I could give them to Myorr. I wanted to model for Phat Farm and could see myself doing it, so I focused on certain things like, what their image is, what is the message Phat Farm says in their national ad campaigns. I took my notes and practiced what I learned for the pictures. I felt great about the pictures, so my friend and I picked out the five pictures we liked. I gave them to Myorr on Monday morning. Myorr asked me, "What's this?"

"They are some pictures I took because I think I have the image you and Russell are looking for in a male model for Phat Farm."

"Okay, I'll take a look at these and let you know, man."

"Thanks, Myorr."

I never heard about those photos. I guess I wasn't the image of "Phat Farm—The American Classic Flava." It didn't stop me though. I knew if I tried hard enough I would make it to a shoot.

You see, as an intern I saw the potential of the internship. I worked a total of five jobs at the time. Little-by-little I pulled away from jobs that were interfering with my internship.

I eventually could put off the waiter and gym training jobs for the weekend or weeknights. I was looking at it like an opportunity to make something more out of this internship. You see, Phat Fashion's doesn't open till 10 a.m. The only person that was there before 10 a.m. was the CFO Rick, or Russell. I knew Rick was at the office everyday at 8:00 a.m. I took advantage of the situation and instead of working a side job early in the morning and then going to NYC, I decided that I should focus all my attention and energy to the job I wanted more.

Every morning the CFO would walk up to the Phat Fashions door to the building, he would find me sitting on the front step waiting to be let in. I noticed a surprised look on his face as he would walk up to find me there waiting. I didn't care. I wanted to be the first one there. My father always taught me to be the first one at your job, show that hunger, and show the bosses and employer it's more than just a job. I watched my father live that saying my whole life.

As an intern I would come into the office and work on whatever Katie had waiting for me. I would make a daily list of what she wanted me to do, and then do each thing one at a time. My father always taught me that if you do something, do it right the first time so you don't have to do it again a second time.

My second name was "Go Get." I related to that name. "Karim, go get that. Karim, go get this." You see, there can never be a job too big for you in the industry. I would get Russell's green juice everyday—fifty times a day if he wanted me to. If Myorr needed me to tape boxes, I did. If Baby Phat employees needed me to run a sample across town on foot, guess what, I did! I was the guy that ran and got whatever whenever. I wasn't trying to suck up to anyone, but I was showing that I can be counted on. And now till this day it all paid off.

Even though I really worked for Katie, she didn't mind me helping others because she saw the potential in me and knew I was more than an intern before I started my internship. Part of my job with Katie was to go to the malls in New York and New Jersey to check up on our two brands, Phat Farm and Baby Phat. We had to see the floor layouts in the major department stores like JC Penny, or Macy's. We would walk in, go to the Phat Farm section of the store, and make sure the department store was maintaining our product nice, clean, and organized. We wanted to make sure Katie's floor designs were being done and that the brand had a great appearance and visual for our consumers. Then we would do the same for Baby Phat.

It's really simple when you're an intern: do your best everyday, show initiative, and don't complain no matter what is being asked of you. Well after about six months of working for Katie at Phat Farm and Baby Phat, I walked in Katie's office because she had asked if she could speak with me. Of course I sat down and wanted to see what was wrong. By the tone of her voice and expression on her face I knew this wasn't a good talk.

"Karim, I think you have been doing a great job here, but I want you to know something before you hear it from someone else. I have decided to leave Phat Fashions to take on other great opportunities that have been offered to me."

"Wow, that's great Katie. So what happens to me?"

"Well Karim, you will most likely work for the person that takes my position. When I resign I will speak highly for you so you don't have to feel like I am abandoning you. I am sorry but these are great opportunities."

"Katie, I completely understand. I am truly happy for you and thankful for the opportunity you gave me."

That night I went home thinking that tomorrow I might no longer have a job at Phat Fashions. I might be living on a park bench again till I can get all four jobs back, working seven days a week. I sat on my coffee table bed looked to the ceiling and said, "God, I thank you for the opportunities you have given me and I thank you for letting me know what it feels like to live the New Yorker life."

The following day I was called into Russell's office. This was the first time Russell specifically asked for me. I had no idea what was going on.

"Hey, Russell!"

"What's up, Karim?"

"Not much . . . you wanted to see me?"

"Yeah, man. Sit down."

So I sat in the chair on the opposite side of him. Russell was sitting at his desk. Seeing all the sneaker designs and sneaker samples all over his desk gave me an idea that he was busy.

"Karim, I'm sure you know about Katie. She's decided to move on and accomplish more goals in her life and I respect her for that and I know she will do great, even though I will deeply miss her."

"Yea, Russ, I spoke with her the other day about it. She warned me that I might not be needed any further and I completely understand that and just wanted to say I appreciate everything you and your Phat Fashions family have taught me."

"Karim, I called you in here to tell you I spoke to Myorr in marketing. We want to give you a shot and let you intern in the marketing and PR department."

"Oh my God, are you serious? I didn't expect this at all, Russ, but I don't know anything about marketing and PR."

"Karim, you didn't know anything about graphic designing and you did that! You can do this! Listen to Myorr, he's the best at what he does. You're young, motivated, and I see that. Trust me, I have faith in you, man."

With a smile on his face Russell continued, "Now get out of my office. I'll see you Monday morning, Homie."

"You got it, Russ! I won't let you down."

That evening on the train ride I went home with an accomplished feeling. My hard work was being seen and starting to pay off. I was laid off a position, but hired to the position I originally wanted. I focused on that goal and here I am going home working for the Godfather of hip hop, doing marketing and PR.

CHAPTER 6

It Was All a Dream

"When you know what you're good at, you make yourself better. "When you discover things you're not good at, you make yourself good." Karim Ramos

So I lost my working relationship with Katie, but gained a job in the marketing and PR department. You see, the marketing and PR department is responsible for marketing the clothing brand Phat Farm and Russell Simmons as a celebrity. Which means placing the brand in major magazines such as GQ, Maxim, even Vogue, and buying national advertisements.

Myorr Janha, vice president of marketing and PR for Phat Farm, simply told me how it works. "Karim, I'm glad to have you on board, man! So the way things work on this side are a little different than Baby Phat or even retail development. What I want you to do is relax! If you need anything, let me know. Take notes if you need to, but all in all, it's pretty chill over here."

I was excited, but nervous, because I can remember sitting at my old desk in Katie's office and peeping my head down the hall and hearing Russell screaming at Kevin or Myorr for something. Or even seeing them grabbing bags of clothes and running down the hall to a photo shoot, video shoot or just for Russell's personal use. For some weird reason, all that hectic-ness, and seeing the guys working really late, got me excited and motivated to really want to be a part of the marketing & PR team!

You see, I wanted the job really bad, so before I met with Myorr that Monday, I "borrowed" and took home a company press kit, which is a backgrounder with historical information on the company. The reason I took that press kit home was to do my homework about Russell Simmons, Phat Farm, and what they stood for. You can't really market or try to promote something you're not familiar with. And it's very hard to promote something you don't believe in. I wanted to get to the root of Phat Fashions. Why did Russell create this brand that was competing against other great brands? So I did some research and homework; now I was ready to learn whatever it was Myorr had for me.

It was another late night, and Myorr, Kevin, and I were putting together the Phat Farm and Baby Phat fashion show. When Myorr designed the men's line for the show, not only did he have to make it look good, but he also had to impress Russell, and also make sure it coordinated with Kimora's Baby Phat clothing line theme. Normally you want to keep the color theme the same in each show. This was my first fashion show so all I could really do was whatever Myorr or Kev told me to do. I noticed everyone played his or her own roles but still worked together as a team. Everything fell into place.

Fashion week is a fashion industry event, lasting approximately one week, which allows fashion designers, brands or "houses" to display their latest collections in runway shows and buyers to take a look at the latest trends. Most importantly, it lets the industry know what's "in" and what's "out" for the season. The most prominent fashion weeks are held in the fashion capitals Milan, London, New York and Paris.

To make a successful fashion show Myorr and Kev would do the following:

1. Choose a venue or a place to hold the event. Make sure there is space for a runway and seating. Choose the time, date and theme of the fashion show, along with Kimora's Baby Phat fashion show.
2. Send out invites.
3. Choose the music which will be the theme of the show. This is when you play the hottest number one songs that will grab the attention of the crowd and move the models as they walk on the runway.
4. Pick out about 30 to 40 complete outfits including hats, sneakers and accessories. We call these samples.

Phat Farm had a lot of licenses, so basically this is the licensee's opportunity to have their "hottest" stuff out in a fashion show to show off their product and boost sales and product placement. Afterwards, the samples are chosen for the show. We start the auditions for male models that have to fit our sample sizes. Sample sizes are normally a large in shirts and 34/33 in jeans or pants. Sample sizes in jackets are. XL and in blazers are a 34R. Calling for a model wasn't that hard. All you have to do is contact modeling agencies, tell them who you were, what kind of models you are looking for, such as, race, age, height, suit size, and shoe size. Then the agency will send you 50 to 100 male models fitting your criteria.

Every day that I hopped on the train to get to NYC always felt like a dream. While listening to my IPOD, I would consider myself a "people watcher" studying folks on the train, their body language, attitudes and facial expressions. Sometimes I'd listen to them complain to someone else on the train about their lives or jobs. But not me! Even though I was living in a basement, sleeping on a coffee table, and driving a very old Oldsmobile that belonged to my mom, I was grateful I was an intern at age 21 working for Russell Simmons. The moment I stepped on the train all my worries and problems were left in Woodbridge, New Jersey. Nobody at Phat Farm or Baby Phat had to know where I lived or what I ate for dinner. I was just grateful. My father always said, "Never bring your problems from home to your work place." Thanks, Dad!

As an intern, I was making ten dollars a day and I was still working on weekends doing security at bars and nightclubs. I needed the money to have a way to work for Russell. I didn't care if I didn't eat. I didn't care if I was sleeping back on that park bench. I was determined to fight through anything as long as I had my internship with Phat Farm. I saw a future with them and all I knew was that I had the potential. I didn't even have a desk to sit at. I worked from a showroom because there was no room in the marketing department. All I had to do was keep my head down and focus on the end result. That coffee table in that cold, old, basement was just a temporary thing. That Oldsmobile I was driving that would run one day and the next day I'd have to run to the train station—was not going to be my car forever. I saw the future. I imagined myself saying, "I work for Russell Simmons and Rev. Run from Run DMC." In the meantime, I couldn't really tell anyone I was an intern because nobody would believe me.

I received news that Phat Farm was moving to a new building. I was nervous because I had no idea what that meant for me or the other interns. All I could do was just help pack up whatever Myorr wanted me to pack. I knew if I did my job the way Myorr showed me, then I would not get let go unless the company couldn't afford me any longer, or no longer needed my assistance.

When I started at Phat Farm, my hectic schedule didn't change much:

4 a.m.—Waking up in a woman's cold, unfinished basement (which was better then the park bench.)

5 a.m.—Training old clients from the gym at their homes.

7 a.m.—Heading to The Big Apple—New York City! Internship for Myorr, Russell, and Phat Farm, working until the last person left the building (even if they left at 10 p.m.)

11 p.m. to 2 a.m.—Security at bars or night clubs.

Weekends were just as busy, just minus NYC and add singing R&B for DJ entertainment companies (such as "Happy Birthday" and another song at the birthday person's request.)

Working so close to Myorr each day was a privilege. I noticed Russell trusted him more than anyone. Myorr was never hated or disrespected. I noticed his calm, cool and relaxed personality was a key to his respect. Myorr always told me to keep my head down and just work. He taught me the "loud" employee was the one Russell didn't acknowledge. He knew Russell since he was a teenager. Myorr worked for Russell when he began the empire Def Jam Records. He went from a receptionist, climbed the ladder of success, never gave up, and ended up becoming Russell's right hand man, leading the brand Phat Farm as the V.P. That was my motivation. I had evidence that if I kept my mouth shut, listened, and took responsibility for my good actions as much as my mistakes things would pay off. Myorr was my living proof that it is possible.

We were at the new building working on another fashion show. It was about midnight and at this point I was used to working late and used to sleeping in the showroom on the nights I didn't have to work at the bars. I assisted Myorr and Kevin on whatever it was they needed from me. One day Russell's assistant said that Russell wanted to see me, but not in his office, in his truck outside the front of the building.

Quizzically, I looked at Myorr and he just gave me a look as if to say he didn't know why. My heart started pounding from the nervousness I was feeling. I didn't know if it was a good or bad thing the big boss man himself wanted me.

I walked down each step, nice and slow, thinking I may have made a mistake, or I was going to get fired. My mind raced 100 miles per hour. I walked to the end of the hallway very slow, hoping someone will pop their head out of the office to say, "Karim, never mind he said it was a mistake." As I'm exiting the building the security guards at the front entrance both said, in unison, "What's up, Karim? I heard Russell's outside waiting for you."

I responded calmly, even though the tempo of my voice was insecure. "Yeah, man, everything's cool."

I walk outside, I see Russell's all black, tinted out, custom made Yukon Denali in front of the building waiting for me—the same all black tinted Denali I saw Russell walking out of my first day as an intern. It was now a year since the last time I sat with Russell alone, when he first when he told me he was giving me a shot in the marketing department, working for Myorr the VP.

I opened the back door to the Denali, sat down and shut the door behind me.

As I was getting comfortable, I looked across from me and I see Russell is on the phone. I'm watching this multimillionaire, dressed so casual, wearing a pair of Phat Farm jeans, fresh white Phat Classics, and simple white Phat Farm polo.

"Okay, Kimora, I like that, let's make that happen. I'll talk to Myorr tomorrow, I love you too . . . bye."

After he hung up with his wife, he said, "What's up, man? How's it going with Myorr and Kev?"

"It's going good, Russ. I can't complain. I've been learning a lot and I appreciate the shot you gave me."

"That's what's up, man. I told you Myorr's the guy you want to work for!"

"Russ, did I do something wrong?" I got more knots in my stomach, like someone punched me.

"Karim, you don't think I know you're the first person at the office and the last person to leave at night?" I didn't know if that was a good thing or bad, so I just looked at Russell with this confused look. Then, suddenly, Russell threw a Motorola Two-Way at my lap.

"Russ, what's this?"

"Karim, welcome to the family! That's your Two-Way . . . you deserve it." My mind went blank, my heart hit the floor, every single tear from when Cheyenne committed suicide to my long, lonely nights crying on a park bench with an empty stomach crossed my mind all in those couple of seconds.

"Russell, man, I'm speechless! Thank you, Russ."

"No, Karim, thank you! I'm going to bring you around the entire company telling everyone that they will be working for you one day." I hugged Russell and told him I wouldn't let him down and that I will continue to work harder.

I went upstairs to Myorr and Kev. They already knew why I was smiling from ear to ear. I hugged Myorr and said "thank you." I told Myorr if there's anything I do wrong or not at his expectations to let me know so I can do it better the next time around. That night I went home on the train a new man. I had accomplished the impossible. I started as an intern with no college, no help, nobody next to me but my goals, God, and my ambition to make it. I was finally an employee at Phat Fashions with a salary and position name. I, Karim Ramos, now worked in the marketing and PR department for Russell Simmons at Phat Farm!

I sat on my coffee table bed that night. The bugs on the floor didn't bother me, the jacket I used to cover myself as a blanket didn't bother me, the smoke coming out of my nose as I breathed because it was so cold didn't bother me. Nothing bothered me that night. I laid down on my coffee table bed in tears of happiness and gratefulness. I cried to God, thanking Him for helping me overcome yet another chapter to my life. Another blessing in disguise!

Maxim Magazine, January 2006

Maxim Magazine, January 2006

Maxim Magazine, January 2006, By Alex Cao

Phat Farm National Ad, By Christian Lantry

One of the great things about classic preppy style is that even though it's sporty and easygoing, it still looks put-together. There's just something about collars and knit patterns. THAT PAGE, clockwise from top left: Ossiery Guy wears a yellow polo by Jockey (more text illegible) over a white polo with gingham collar by Ryan Seacrest ($98). His jacket jeans are by Chip & Pepper ($150). Dangling Runt is in a striped polo by NY Based ($48) and jeans by Seacrest jeans ($75). Shy Guy's polo is by Paul Frank ($86). His dark-wash jeans are by Chip & Pepper ($86). Pockets wears a polo by Rocawear ($86) and heated-pocket pants by Rocawear ($75). THIS PAGE: Look out for our cooler's right hook. He's in a navy jacket ($275), plaid pants ($225) and yellow herringbone shirt ($140), all by Sean John. His silk and cashmere sweater-vest is by Iceberg ($350) and his striped tie is by Paul Smith Accessories ($125). The ring girl is in a red bustier with black lace trim by Cosabella (more text illegible) and a tube dress by House of Field ($1,200). Our Rocky, brandishing the left uppercut, is in a seersucker blazer ($588) and matching pants ($220) by Paul Smith. The lime green shirt ($350) and lavender V-neck sweater ($340) are also by Ryan Seacrest. Paul Smith accessories makes his tie ($125). By the way, you'll probably want to ground all the colors and patterns with neutral-color shoes. These clothes take life on preppy hallmarks—collegiate looks, upper-crusty fabrics and textures—and marry them to contemporary notions of comfort and style. A kind of hip-hop sangfroid that amounts to the classic, for instance.

Playboy Magazine, February 2005, By Rick Rock

p r e p's

Break out the khaki and polos—it's time to go back to the 1980s

He struggles in a northside three-button blazer with elbow patches ($475), striped shirt ($86) and faded denim pants ($98) all by Paul Frank. (Check out the contrasting blue collar on the shirt.) His fedora is by Paul Smith Accessories ($240). His sunspot is in a medium dress by Rinetti ($670). So subtle wears a center two-button blazer ($350), his single sweater ($75) and shorts ($85), all by Paul Frank. His hat is also by Paul Smith Accessories ($240).

Playboy Magazine, February 2005, By Rick Rock

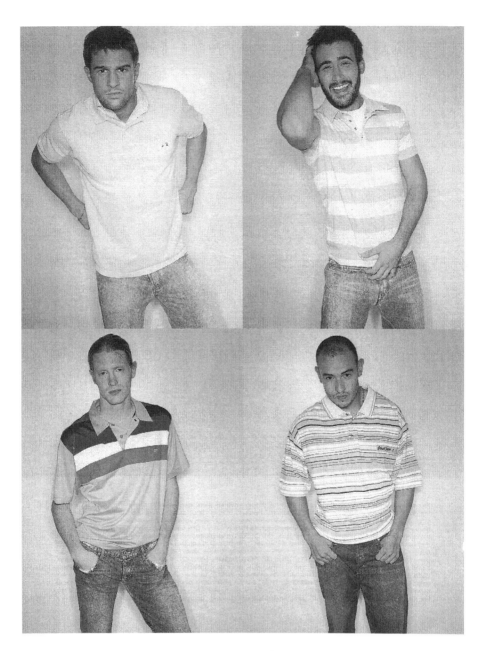

Playboy Magazine Editorial

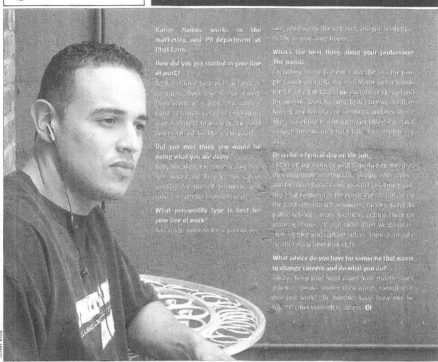

Karim Ramos works in the marketing and PR department at Phat Farm.

How did you get started in your line of work?

Did you ever think you would be doing what you are doing?

What personality type is best for your line of work?

What's the best thing about your profession? the worst?

Describe a typical day on the job.

What advice do you have for someone that wants to change careers and do what you do?

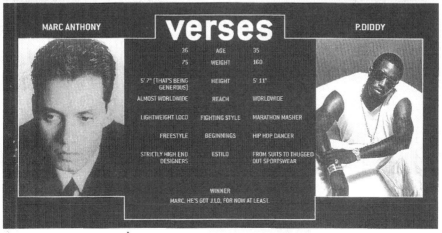

MARC ANTHONY	verses	P.DIDDY
36	AGE	35
75	WEIGHT	160
5' 7" (THAT'S BEING GENEROUS)	HEIGHT	5' 11"
ALMOST WORLDWIDE	REACH	WORLDWIDE
LIGHTWEIGHT LOCO	FIGHTING STYLE	MARATHON MASHER
FREESTYLE	BEGINNINGS	HIP HOP DANCER
STRICTLY HIGH END DESIGNERS	ESTILO	FROM SUITS TO THUGGED OUT SPORTSWEAR
	WINNER	
	MARC. HE'S GOT J.LO, FOR NOW AT LEAST.	

Phat Farm Ad, 2003

My Comp Card

Me & Myorr

Me & R&B Sensation Mya @ Hev Performance in NJ

Me & Russell Simmons in Miami, FL
(Who would have thought I'd be modeling for him?)

Me (as an intern), Russell Simmons, Brian Ward, & Kevin Liles

Me, Swizz Beatz, & DJ Khalid

The Commission: Me, Myorr Janha, Kevin "Dogg" Jones, & Treis Hill
(Bel Todmann and Rasheed Young were not available this night.)

Me & Hip Hop Artist Fat Joe @ His Baby Shower

Kool Cig Ad

Kool Cig Ad

Me & Hip Hop Artist and Actor LL Cool J @ Fat Joe's Baby Shower

Me & Russell Simmons @ Photo Shoot

Smile, Cheyenne, you're finally famous!

Who would have known I would have been on a billboard?

Me & Mom

Me & Motivational Speaker and Author Depak Chopra

Me & My Best Friend and Little Brother Rodrigo Carrera

CHAPTER 7

Play Your Position

*"Either you're playing in the game . . . or you're watching the game,
but you can't be doing both." Karim Ramos*

My phone rings at 8 a.m.

"Hello, this is Karim."

"Hey, Karim! It's Monica."

"Hey, what's up, Monica?"

"LL Cool J has a Gatorade commercial coming up tomorrow. I'm sorry I didn't call you in advance."

"I got you, we have his sizes on file so let me work on it. I'll talk to Myorr and see what we can get for him."

"Thank you, Karim! I will definitely make sure Phat Farm gets some shine!"

"You always do, Monica. Trust me, Russell and Myorr appreciate all the *shine and love you give us."

After speaking with Monica, I immediately called Myorr.

"Myorr, what's up man?"

"What's up, Karim?"

"Well I just got a call from Monica and she needs gear for a Gatorade commercial by tomorrow. I checked our stash of clothes already and we have a couple outfits."

"Okay, so have Monica pick up that stuff you have for him and then let LL go to the Phat Farm store in Soho, New York with Monica to get three more outfits and let him keep them all after the shoot."

"Got it, Myorr, okay see you later."

About an hour later Russell walks into my office.

"What's up, Karim?"

"Not much Russ, just got a call about an hour ago. LL has a Gatorade commercial and Monica's pulling for him so Myorr wants me to give him what we have here and let him go to our store to pick some other stuff."

"Karim, get him a lot of options, go to the store yourself and pick some "Fly" stuff. Meet him at his shoot and hang out with him and get him to rock some nice Phat Farm Gear."

"Okay, no problem. I'll call Monica and get the info."

That day I ended up getting LL Cool J about 10 outfits from head to toe. I met with Monica the next day and got to hang with LL and watch him train. My daily schedule went from just doing anything I was told to do to, and also squeezing the following:

* Check all my voice messages in the morning. Myorr always told me to make sure I call every single person back, even if we couldn't help him or her. That way nobody could ever say to Myorr or Russell that they called and never received a call back.
* Cleaning up the showroom and putting back all the samples that were previously pulled for a video, or photo shoot.
* Check the fax machine for requests. I would average about 10 different requests daily. Depending on the value of the shoot and the chances of being able to actually see our Phat Farm logo would determine how much clothes would be given.

For instance, I would give more clothes to a *Vibe* magazine shoot, or *Maxim* magazine, or *XXL* magazine or even *GQ* magazine because the apparel (product placement) would be used for editorial—when a magazine shoots our clothes on models for consumers to buy.

I would wait untill Myorr got in to discuss who was requesting what to make sure I gave clothes to those he and Russell thought were top priority. Myorr worked out a promotional tour with Phat Farm and Baby Phat sponsored by Motorola and Anheuser Bush (Budweiser), that way the partnership was a cross promotion between the four brands to help sales for each brand. This promotional tour consisted of radio and television interviews with Russell Simmons, Rev Run (*Run's House*) and Kimora Lee Simmons, followed by in-store signings. T-shirts and sneakers were given away to the first 500 people who attended the "after-parties" at various night clubs. My job was to make sure that the party giveaways were successfully delivered to Myorr's hotel and head shots of Russell and Rev Run were delivered to the store for them to sign and distribute to their fans and supporters.

At this point my responsibilities were growing by the day. The dream was settling in and becoming a reality. I realized my life was becoming my work. The meaning of "Karim Time" was nothing but a figment of my imagination. A relationship with a woman was impossible. "Trust me, Karim, I understand your job and will support you in everything you do" was a fib that I was tired of hearing. I didn't get to see my family for about three years because work was my life. I felt that I had to learn and do everything I could to succeed at working in the marketing department.

Everyday was an exciting, eventful day. I would still wake up at 3 a.m. to go to the gym, come home and shower, then run to the station to catch the 7:15 a.m. train, just so I made sure to be the first one at the office. Now and then I'd talk to friends of mine, hear how good their lives were and how big their houses were. And here I was, still waking up in a dark, cold, wet basement room. I grew tired of sleeping in an un-finished basement with a humidifier in my face; and got more upset every time I used my old leather jacket as a blanket to keep me warm at night. Sleeping on the coffee table began to hurt my back.

The stench of mildew and using my cell phone as a flashlight to get to the other side of the room to turn the light on was making me aggravated. Between walking around in my 99-cent store flip flops to prevent stepping on an insect and the little shower in the corner with a garden hose, I was going crazy! I was happy and thankful but for some reason I kept hearing my father's words, "Son, there's always a straw that breaks the camels back." His words stalked me each morning.

I looked in the newspaper and online for an apartment. I had to find one with all utilities included. About a week later I found myself living in a finished basement in Avenel, NJ for $600 a month, all utilities included. This was a major step up for me going from the park bench to the old UN-finished basement, to a basement apartment that had my own bathroom, kitchen, and living room. I didn't mind the loneness or even the wood paneled walls. The feeling of being able to call something mine was all I wanted.

Buying personal items at flea markets and garage sales brought me back to the shopping days with Dad. Sometimes when I did not agree with Dad, he still taught me that all that matters is surviving the struggles of life. At the end of the day if my sofa and TV were found in the garbage or bought from a garage sale, I always thought about what Dad told me, "One man's junk is another man's treasure." I wasn't ashamed to admit it. I knew it wasn't forever and I knew this was just a stepping-stone till the day I could walk into Best Buy to buy a brand new TV or a new bed like everyone else!

Everyday I was very positive at Phat Fashions. It always felt like another first day to me. Not being able to see my mother for a long time or hang out with friends didn't faze me, I kept my personal problems at home just like my dad taught me.

Sleeping in Russell's office, on his leather custom-made sofa, was a deep secret I wouldn't dare tell anyone. I slept on the sofa when I had deadlines to make for Myorr or when I wanted to get an early start on things. I would wake up before anyone got to the office in the morning, run to my desk and grab my toothbrush, toothpaste and soap and wash my face. At times I would even use Russell's shower, wash up real quick and keep on going like it never happened. One day I saw Russell down the hall as I'm making my "Good morning!" stops.

"Karim, stop by my office when you get a second," Russ said.

"Okay, Russ," I replied.

I had no idea what he could have possibly wanted. I was a little nervous because I thought maybe he found out I was sleeping on his sofa in his office or something.

"Russ, what's up man? You wanted to see me?" I asked.

"Yeah, get in here man."

I sat down across from him and waited till he was off the phone with Kimora. He hangs up.

"Russ, what's up man?"

"Steve Lobel is going on tour with Bone Thugs & Harmony. It's going to be a 15 city tour and Myorr asked me what I thought about you going with them. I think it would be a good experience for you," he stated.

"Okay Russ, thanks! I'll take pictures of the infamous hip hop group in Phat Farm. I'll get some giveaways from Myorr for some fans, and I'll set up a table for your energy drink Def Con 3."

It was truly an amazing feeling walking out of LAX Airport in Los Angeles, CA by myself. I grabbed my bags and saw a brand new tour bus that had the words "Phat Farm" wrapped around it with the name of the group and tour. I met with Steve Lobel and Bone Thugs N Harmony. I was welcomed by this amazing and talented group as if they knew me for years.

I set the road on a two-week tour with the group—city to city, hotel to hotel. Everything was amazing: the sold-out concerts, the fans and the music. I sat on stage taking pictures of the group as they performed with Phat Farm clothing on in every city. I met with hundreds of fans as I gave away posters of Rev Run and his newly released Hampton sneaker, t-shirts, and Russell's energy drink Def Con 3.

Traveling for two weeks with a group that I used to listen to when I was in high school, getting to actually listen to each guys personal story, laugh with them, and see them touch thousands of fans in 10 different cities was absolutely amazing. And it gets better! The group had a recording studio in the back of the tour bus and I was asked to record with the group singing background to their original songs and to some new songs. I couldn't believe it! Here I was singing with one of the infamous rap groups I used to sing to with my brother when he was alive. Here I was on tour with them. In a couple cities I even got out on stage and got to sing "Happy Birthday" to a couple women with the group backing me up! A feeling I can never forget, the rush of having the attention of thousands! Thank you, Steve Lobel and Bone Thugs N Harmony.

My responsibilities were building. My work was finally paying off. I went on tours, and I went with Russell to shows in NYC. I was helping Myorr get press for Russell as they all traveled the world. Even though I really wanted to travel with Russell, his brother Rev Run and Myorr, I always kept Myorr's advice in the back of my head, "Keep your head down, and your mouth shut, Karim. In time Russell will see what you do and so will everyone else. So many people hate on you as it is because you're young, have a title and already traveling on the road for the company."

I noticed in the fashion and music business somebody always wants your position. That's why I was always the first in the office and the last to leave. It got to the point Russell would come into the office or just call my desk asking me what was going on with the brand or to make sure I send clothes to someone he promised free clothes to. Here I was walking into the building one day when Russell stopped me and asked about the outfit I was wearing.

"What's up, Karim? We have those jeans and shirt in the office?"

"What's up, Russ? Yeah, we have it up stairs."

"Go grab me that same outfit in my sizes and bring it downstairs, you're coming with me."

"Okay, Russ."

So I ran upstairs as if I was in a marathon 'cause I didn't want the boss to wait. I ran back down with a complete outfit and a couple extra shirts all in Russell's sizes just incase he changes his mind.

Here I was in Russell's all black Denali. I sent Myorr a message letting him know I was with Russell and that I had no idea where he was taking me.

Myorr responded, "You're going with him to a Panasonic commercial he's in."

My heart dropped when Russell said to me, "You're my stylist today man, so make me look fresh."

I had his outfit he requested and it's a good thing I brought a couple extra outfits, because Russell likes to have variety. We pulled up to the commercial shoot. I saw Russell's assistant Simone, Rev Run, and a bunch of production staff. The room was set up a mimic of our sneaker showroom at Phat Farm. I went to the back room with Russell and steamed all the outfits I hand picked out for him.

"What you got for me, Karim?"

"I got you four outfits, Russ."

"They all look fly! Give me this one and save the outfit you have on for the next shot."

Here I was, dressing Russell Simmons for a Panasonic commercial—the guy who made fun of me for wearing corny clothes when he was an intern, is now dressing the godfather of hip hop! I was amazed and overwhelmed with all the cameras, the people working on the commercial and the director screaming, "Quiet everyone! Action!"

I went back to the office that night with Russell and even though I felt good about helping, I heard people in the building were bothered, and upset that I was invited to the shoot and not them. I call them "haters." I noticed the more involved I got in the company the more people wanted to hold me down and try to make me look bad so credit I deserved was not given to me. In a situation like this I remembered Myorr's advice, people will hate on me, so all I can do is brush my shoulder and keep moving forward.

With all my responsibilities Myorr thought I could handle the responsibility of booking Russell and Rev Run for morning show radio and television visits across the nation while they continue their sneaker promotional tour. Basically for every city Russell and Rev. Run held an in-store promotional signing, my job was to establish relationships with the town's local radio and TV morning show producers to promote why the two celebrities were in town.

These promotions increased the number of fans and supporters that came to the scheduled in-store signing to receive their autographed pictures from Russell and Rev. Run. These in-store appearances not only promoted the brands (Phat Farm and Baby Phat), but it also gave many people the opportunity to express their ideas, goals, and questions regarding fashion, music, or film industries. Many people even came to seek spiritual consulting and guidance. On the average, in-store signings reached out to anywhere from 1000 to 5000 hearts, minds, and souls. The responsibility of creating Russell and Rev. Run's itinerary for over 40 cities a year was almost like a dream.

Remembering the struggle I took from sleeping on a park bench, and wanting to kill myself over my own failures brought thoughts of my beloved brother Cheyenne. I really felt I could have saved him if I had read between the lines in his messages. I realize I wouldn't be where I was and where I was going to if I would have given up!

In about two years of serving Phat Farm and making it my priority and continuing my hard work, ideas, and devotion I received a text from Myorr.

"We need to talk. Let's meet up for lunch tomorrow around one p.m."

With that kind of text from Myorr I couldn't help but respond with, "Is everything okay?"

He replied, "Yeah."

Myorr isn't known to have long descriptive text messages. They are normally one or two words without emotion or feeling, which leaves the mind wondering what he is really trying to say. That night I probably slept about an hour from being so nervous on what Myorr wanted to speak to me about. The next day came, I went to the gym as always, went home, showered, and got to work early as normal. One o'clock couldn't come any sooner. We met at this Japanese restaurant by our office.

"What's up, Myorr?"

"Not much, you know same old same old."

"So what's going on? You okay?

"Yep, everything is great." My heart felt relief that very second.

"Karim, I've been talking with Russ and I want you to take over the public relations side of Phat Farm for Russell. I want you to be the director of PR and work with all of Russell's other publicists that coordinate his calendar so that you guys are all on the same page and can make Russell's schedule flow smooth." I'm sure even though I tried my best to hide my happiness from Myorr, he could see it in my face that I was excited about the promotion.

"Myorr, I'll do whatever you guys need me to do. I will coordinate with the other publicist and make sure we can get Russ the most press for every city without wearing him out."

"Karim, best of all, you are going on the road with us for our new Phat Farm and Baby Phat tour. It's about thirty cities, so get your passport and stuff. You will be responsible for coordinating Russell and Rev. Runs daily itinerary, booking their radio and TV press, distributing the itinerary to the right people in the company, and helping me with the in-store signing and after party club venue set ups we do for every city . . . I know you won't let me down."

That night I went back home on the train knowing that when I wake up the next day I will be the Director of Public Relations for Phat Farm and Russell Simmons. I was living the slogan Russell lived by—"The American Dream".

* NOTE: "Shine and Love" is when an artist or their stylist gets our Phat Farm product in their videos or photo shoots to help increase sales and drive fans to wear what their icon or favorite celebrity is wearing. In this case Monica is LLCool J's personal stylist and she's pulling for LL who will be in a Gatorade commercial.

CHAPTER 8

Oh So Focused

"Appreciate your life, stay humble, and put God first." Karim Ramos

"Hello, Mr. Ramos, my name is Pete and we have to get you to Teterboro Airport."

Wait a minute, am I really here catching a car service ride to a private jet airport? I pinched myself at least two times. I couldn't believe I was the fat kid that was told he would never amount to anything, the same fat kid that didn't see a future for himself and thought suicide was the solution. The same kid that would go to bed on an empty stomach is now catching a car service ride to the private airport to fly out with Russell Simmons and Rev. Run. Sitting in the back of a tinted Towns Car, with a driver in the front who is apologizing to me for the bumper to bumper traffic!

I knew I was no Russell Simmons, or P Diddy, or Jay Z, but I just couldn't believe what was going on. Here I am traveling with the godfather of hip hop, Russell Simmons and his brother Rev. Run from the legendary group Run DMC. I would have never imagined this in my life especially being that Run DMC was my brothers favorite group. All this because I never gave up!

Russell's entourage consisted of a small group of us, besides just him and his right hand man Gary. The team we had we called "The Commission." The Commission was a group of us that flew together. Myorr was the captain, and then you had Kev Dogg, Bel, Rasheed, Treis, then me. We all worked together to make sure Russell, Rev. Run, or even Kimora had everything they wanted from morning show press, to a full house in-store signing promoting their product, to a full house promotional after party later that evening. We all had our own responsibilities so we worked as a team as we traveled all over the world. Myorr was the head of the group, yet he was always the humblest. I realized I could learn so much from Myorr and Russell.

At the in-store events with Russell and Rev. Run I would roll up Rev Run's poster after he autographed them for the fans and supporters that attended the in-store event. I always liked to analyze my superior's actions and reactions. I always liked to stand back and study Russell, Rev. Run, and Myorr. Russell was so humble and giving that anyone who hung out with him would feel the same. I would watch hundreds of people in almost 50 different cities approach Russell with a different story, seeking advice, asking for an autograph, or just wanting to shake the hands of a mogul for good luck. For every single fan Russell encountered with, he never once turned anyone down. He always listened, spoke, and gave the best advice that he could.

I remember so many people had the same idea that I had at one point, which was that they wanted to be a singer, or actor, or model, or just work in the entertainment business. Russell's response always was honest and useful. He would tell them, "If you want to be a model, singer, or actor, you have to be in the industry with a specific goal. You can't live in Montana if you want to be an actor or model or singer. You have to move to a major city like New York or L.A. You have to make friends and rub elbows with those in the same field as your goals. Like if you wanted to be an attorney then make friends with people studying law. Intern at a law firm and serve with a humble heart."

Listening to Russell give that advice reminded me of the risk and challenge I faced the day I left Ocala, FL to pursue music and the entertainment business. I risked it all to the point where I had no place to live or food to eat for a period of time. I eventually made it all because I saw what I wanted and kept striving for it. In the back of my mind I always said the struggle was temporary. Never give up!

Our flight arrangement changed about three times regarding what airport, what flight, and if it was a private jet or commercial flight. Part of my job is to make sure that everyone traveling with Russell gets an updated itinerary. Well in the last hour Russell's assistant changed the flight info to leave out of the private airport. So meanwhile everyone is on their way to the commercial airport, we all had to make U-turn to catch the private jet before a certain time. I immediately jumped on my Blackberry to start emailing everyone the new flight information. The mistake I made was I emailed everyone except Russell's right hand man, Gary. When we all got to the private airport I immediately reached out to Gary and told him where we were and what time the jet was taking off. I apologized repeatedly for not having the information for him sooner like everyone else. Gary wasn't bothered. He said he was on his way to the private jet.

When Russell arrives we normally all just get on the jet so that he doesn't have to wait for anyone. This time it was different. Russell was ready to go, but the jet also had to leave at a certain time or our flight would leave the next day. Because of Russell's crazy tour schedule and press that was already booked by me, it was imperative that we get on this last flight. The pilots came out to us and said we have to take off.

I yelled, "We have one more person!"

At this time Russell could tell I was stalling the flight departure waiting for Gary, so I had to tell Russell the truth that I made a mistake and didn't include Gary on the recipient list. Russell was extremely upset with me and very disappointed. The doors shut . . . my heart drops. Our flight was exiting the runway, getting ready for take off as Gary was stepping onto the runway. I looked out my window and I see Gary with his luggage. I immediately looked at Myorr and just repeatedly apologized for my mistake. Myorr was always calm, no matter how difficult or hard the situation was. He looked at me and said, "You just have to take responsibility for your actions Karim. We all make mistakes." This was one flight I knew Russell wanted me to get off and walk to our destination to teach me a lesson. I kept my mouth shut and just tried to focus on the rest of the trip.

We landed at the airport and Gary landed 20 minutes after us, he caught a flight with some business owners that dropped him off. Here I was working on another fashion show, carrying more responsibilities for Myorr. We get ready for Phat Farm &

Baby Phat's big 10-year anniversary fashion show that was being held at Bryant Park in New York City. While I was interviewing the models for the fashion shows, I came across Channing Tantum, who was originally from Florida like me. We clicked pretty quickly. When I asked him how long he has been modeling, he said, "Years." I told him I'd like to model one day and he told me that I should look into it and try it. He told me how its easy money. Channing was done with the modeling pretty much and wanted to get into acting. Years later, he became a star actor in *G.I. Joe*. I'm very proud of him. I lost his contact number, but I wish him the best.

Every night for about two weeks we were working in the office till about 2 a.m. Catered food was pretty much something I got used to, except this year I found myself being hand fed Hush Puppies from Tyra Banks, the famous model, actress, and host from her hit show *America's Next Top Model*.

"Have you ever had a Hush Puppy, Karim?"

"No."

"Here, try one." Tyra dipped this little brown fried dough ball in a sweet sauce and fed me.

"Wow! Tastes good!"

"Have another sweetie."

"Wow, they are good," I said, with a flirting tone in my voice.

She gives me another one. Now I can't believe that *the* Tyra Banks is hand feeding me, so I was enjoying the moment like there was no tomorrow.

"Karim! Stop flirting with Tyra!" Russell screamed with a smile on his face.

I looked at Russell and said, "I wasn't flirting, just trying new food."

He said, "Stop flirting with Ming's [his first born daughter] godmother."

Tyra couldn't help but laugh and walk away. Thanks, Russell!

That year we had an incredible fashion show with both Phat Farm and Baby Phat. And I was a part of it. Outside of the Phat Fashions Empire I became really good friends with Steve Lobell. Wherever there was a music industry event, there was Steve Lobell. Steve grew up with Russell Simmons, Run DMC and Fat Joe. I ran with Steve for years in the streets. I've met so many celebrities through Steve. I remember we went to Diddy's house in NYC, AKA P. Diddy's Bad Boy Records.

Here I was listening to a beat that R&B artist Carl Tomas was working on. Steve walked in the studio session saying, "What's up?" and just started talking to Carl. It was about 2:30 a.m. as P. Diddy walked in and said hello to all of us. Diddy was in an optimistic positive mood, as he's looking to Carl he says, "Let's get this Carl! Make those hits!" I said hello to Diddy and asked him if he ever sleeps. I told him he reminds me of Russell. He looked at me and said, "Reem, sleep when you're dead." Then he walked out. I took those words of wisdom and realized here is P. Diddy Combs, Russell Simmons, and Steve Lobel, all men who have their own businesses. They have well established relationships and employees by the hundreds that work for them yet they are up at night working, networking, and meeting people when everyone else in the world is sleeping. They are so humble and love to serve. That's what I want, to serve 24 hours a day, seven days a week.

When I had surgery on both of my feet, my doctor had made me take off from work for a month to heal. During that month I was driving to the city to meet up with

Steve Lobel to jump into different studio sessions. I recorded back-up vocals for Bone Thugs N Harmony, met with different artists such as hip hop rapper Fat Joe or hip hop rapper/producer Jim Jones. I didn't want to stop so if I wasn't at Phat Fashions then I was traveling to video sets and recording studios with Steve.

If I was off on weekends from Phat Farm, I'd travel to L.A. to meet up with Steve and his crew and hit up different movie sets and video shoots. One day I'd be on set with director Bret Ratner directing pop sensation Jessica Simpson's new video. Another day I'd be with my very close friend Jessy Terrero watching him direct videos from 50 Cent to Fat Joe. It was like this for years. I wanted to see the lifestyle, study the culture of hip hop, and be a part of history.

I remember sitting on Brand Jordan's yacht party that was featuring the new Carmelo Antony basketball sneakers. On the yacht I was with hip hop's Suge Knight, Mystical, DMC (from Run DMC), Steve Lobel, and others. The following day after the yacht party, I attended the Hip Hop Vibe awards where Myorr and I organized a Phat Farm fashion show. Russell received the Life Time Achievement Award that evening. Here I was 25-years-old, traveling all over the world, working for Russell Simmons and Rev. Run, plus, working on my own side projects such as my music with Steve Lobell.

I tried to serve and give back so I joined Russell Simmons' Arts for Life Foundation, which is an organization that Russell and his brother Danny Simmons put together years ago. It was a way to give back to the unfortunate. I would help the organization by setting up their benefit they held every year at Russell and Kimora's house in the Hamptons. This benefit was held twice a year and gave any celebrity or artist the opportunity to give back by buying things that were auctioned off. Stars like from Chevy Chase to the girls from *Sex in the City* to hip hop legend LL Cool J, all attended. Steve and I created a one of a kind automatic chopper, designed with the Beverly Hills Chopper founder. It was a Phat Farm and Baby Phat chopper that each got auctioned off for $15K. I enjoyed helping every year even when Arts for Life went to West Palm Beach, FL at Donald Trump's estate, mingling with everyone from Donald Trump to Dwayne "The Rock" Johnson or even baseball's legendary Sammy Sosa.

Arts for Life always scheduled Russell to do positive motivational speeches to all these groups and schools. I took part with Myorr and Russell to help motivate the youth. Arts For Life always found it more influential when you have someone young like myself talking to young minds that may need guidance, or help finding their path to life. I could relate to these college kids and students. We were basically the same age, if not I was younger in a lot of situations.

I would always think about how I could give back, to show God I appreciate everything he's given me. I knew that just like everything was going great for me, in a snap of a finger, it could all be taken away. I decided to speak to colleges, universities, small special groups, and the less fortunate high schools. I even went out of my way to speak to schools in struggling cities throughout New York. Those children motivated me more then life itself because they were less fortunate. I would let the students know right from the start that I wasn't paid to be there, I was there because I wanted to help.

I had one situation where a student gave me a hard time and told me that everything that happened to me was pure luck. He reminded me of myself when I was younger with a negative attitude. I saw in his eyes that he was lost. No father, no mother, being watched by an aunt that that was never home. He learned how to cook at the age of 7 to survive in his house and help his younger brother. He faced more responsibilities at the age of 10 then the average man at the age of 18. I admired him and told him that I can relate in one way or another.

I would normally give my e-mail address to the students I speak to at these engagements to answer any questions, give advice, or even if it's just words of motivation they want to hear from me. With this one young man, I gave him my personal cell phone number and even my home address. I taught him everything from what I've learned on my own, to the lessons taught to me by Russell or Myorr or Rev. Run.

I received a letter from this particular student about three years later telling me he moved into a house in Florida with his wife, his new born child, and he even took his younger brother with him all while he attended a four-year university and was a supervisor at a pharmaceutical company. Derek, I am proud of you and you did this all on your own by just believing in yourself and never giving up!

One day we had a Phat Farm and Baby Phat brunch that we held in our showroom on the 43rd floor of our office. This event was designed to service all of our magazine stylists, personal celebrity stylists, movie stylists and video stylists. We basically wanted stylists to come and see the new line of clothes. But instead of sending them just a book with all the information, we decided to do a brunch where they can actually see the apparel themselves and converse with us on what needed to be improved. But better yet, this was an opportunity for Russell to meet the people who support the brand by using the apparel for their photo shoots. A good 150 to 200 people came to look at the clothing lines and enjoy the personal massages on our 43rd floor suite. We all enjoyed the champagne, and the personal chef that cooked any kind of omelet you wanted. Among the crowd there was a gentleman by the name of Joseph DeAcetis.

Joseph DeAcetis was the fashion director of *Playboy* magazine. I knew Joseph for being so popular and well respected in the fashion industry. Joseph and I normally just spoke about Phat Farm. He liked when I put the outfits together myself because there was a storyline behind my outfits and he liked the final look. At the brunch, I was sitting next to Russell eating an egg white omelet and just talking about upcoming trips we had to look forward to, when all of a sudden Joseph approached Russell and I and said, "Karim, do you model?"

Russell, spoke before I was able to and said, "Karim, a model? He ain't no freaking model."

I turned to Russell and with laughter behind my voice and said, "Come on man, Russell, can I live? Geez . . . the man wants me to model."

Russell looked at me laughing and said, "You ain't no model man."

I looked at Joseph and told him, that Russell was actually right and that I was no model.

Joseph said, "Karim, let's do one shoot and if I don't like your shots, then I won't use you. I think you have a very good, but different and distinct look."

I said, "Oh, I am definitely not going to turn you down and say no! I will be there. Tell me when and where and I'm there."

Later that night I received an e-mail from Joseph's assistant that said:

Karim,

> *We are so excited that you are going to be a part of our next issue in Playboy! Here's the information you will need.*
> *Milk Studios*
> *NYC*
> *8 a.m. start*
> *See you there, can't wait! You're going to look fabulous!*

Regards,
Korin, Assistant to Joseph DeAcetis
Fashion Department
Playboy Magazine

How is it possible that my brother Cheyenne who modeled, won beauty pageants, and looked incredible, took his own life by suicide when he had so much potential to grow and better himself from these life long lessons that are thrown at us? Yet here I am, this kid who used to weigh 262 pounds, was lacking motivation, always thinking negative, be working for Russell Simmons and now being offered a shot at modeling for an international magazine that's been around since I was a born . . . *Playboy* magazine?!

All I could think of was appreciating God and realizing how important it is to NEVER GIVE UP!

CHAPTER 9

The Sky's the Limit

"Life is not a matter of having good cards, but of playing a poor hand well . . . At the end of the day, play what GOD gives you & appreciate it ALL AS YOU WIN OR LOSE! The game isn't over till YOU SURRENDER and turn in the cars. Keep playing . . . stay in the GAME of LIFE! Karim Ramos

After landing that *Playboy* magazine shoot, so many other doors opened up for me in the modeling business. I had fellow employees at Phat Fashions who doubted me and said the first photo shoot I had with *Playboy* was out of luck, even though it did lead me to three more Playboy issues. Russell was not really accepting the fact that I was modeling on the side, and I could understand why. So to show my loyalty to Russell and Phat Farm I made sure every photo shoot I did I was wearing Phat Farm or another male model had on Phat Farm. I wanted Russell to feel I was still loyal to his brand, even though he never ever told me I had to wear Phat Farm in my photo shoots.

Then one day the unexpected happened, I received my first copy of *Playboy* magazine. It was sent to my office and put on my desk. It was the February 2005 issue and I picked it up and opened it to see the editorial section. I wanted to check if Phat Farm got any shine. As I opened to the first page, my colleague Tamisha, who was the VP of the kids department for Phat Farm and Baby Phat Kids, walked in and yelled, "Oh, Mr. Ramos!" She was holding the very same issue in her hands with a smile from ear to ear.

I said, "What's up, T?"

"Mr. Ramos, or should I say, Mr. Snuggles, did you see yourself?"

I laughed. Then with nervousness in my tone I said, "Mr. Snuggles, what's that mean?"

Sure enough when I opened to the editorial section of the magazine, I saw pages with pictures of me. I couldn't believe it! I felt numb! I was so shocked and excited! Words can't even describe the feeling. I smiled and read the description underneath one of the pictures. They called me "Mr. Snuggles." I didn't know how to act. I mean here was a kid who was made fun of his whole life about his weight or big ears and now my six pack was illustrated in an international magazine that was distributed all over the world. I went home that night riding the train so excited and shocked that all I could keep doing was thanking God for this opportunity.

I didn't want to tell my family just yet, it was too good to be true so I kept my mouth shut and tried not to jinx myself in hopes that I will do more photo shoots. The next day I walked into Russell's office to clean out and reorganize his closet and clothes in his bathroom. I saw the *Playboy* magazine issue lying on his desk. I didn't want to say anything, so I did what I had to do and left. As I was walking out Russell was coming in and, with a smirk on his face, he said, "I saw your pictures, niggy. What you think you're a model now?"

I replied, "Nope, just working, trying to get Phat Farm shine." He never really congratulated me. It didn't bother me at all; I just kept doing what I had to do.

After that photo shoot, I landed other shoots with magazines, small up-coming Italian clothing companies and test shoots. I was even as a fit model, where they use my body as a mold to create their apparel for the customer so every pair of size 34 jeans are the same size and every large shirt is the same. All these opportunities were coming to me little-by-little and running around the world with Russell and with Myorr was just a dream come true. Myorr always congratulated me on what I did as a model on the side. I always came to him as a friend. He was my boss but more like my big brother. I knew Myorr would never steer me in the wrong direction. I knew he loved me in a family way. I always knew if I wanted to be successful like him in the industry all I had to do was always consult with him.

My responsibilities continued to grow by the day. I even had the privilege of dressing Russell for different events and award ceremonies. It was a privilege since I was once the kid who was made fun of years ago for my shoes, pants, and ties—and I now ended up exploring fashion to another level. Getting a call from Russell at 8a.m., asking me to get him three outfits and to choose the best one for a particular event almost became routine. We even had our moments where I would have to change my outfit because Russell and I looked like twins! Hey, he's the boss, so whatever he wears you want to make sure you don't look like his twin.

Some days I would be traveling with Russell to different recording studios so that he could record a promotional commercial of his brand of clothing for different department stores to air. Then, next thing I knew, I was with Steve Lobel going to my own studio sessions to work on songs that Steve gathered beats for me to write to. One day on the jet with Russell landing in Chicago, then in Miami, then Atlanta . . . There were days we flew to two different cities in one day. In between the traveling I would run and do auditions for a magazine or commercials.

Normally we would come back from our Phat Farm tour on a Sunday, go to Russell's house to watch *The Soprano's* on HBO or just to hang out and relax, then back at the office Monday morning and work on our weekly project for the clothing brand, then head back out to the private airport on Wednesday to continue our promotional tour. Whenever our tours were done for that season, I would take every opportunity and chance that was given to me to audition or do photo shoots for different brands.

Every year for about three years I would travel to Las Vegas with Myorr and a magazine company called *Stuff* magazine, to throw a fashion show and party at the Palms Casino Resort. This event was created by *Stuff* magazine to basically get their magazine involved in the urban world and cross the line. It was great for Phat Farm and Baby Phat because we were able to connect with another great market. Whenever we traveled for this event it was my birthday. And every year Myorr did the same thing, we would go to dinner with the main crew involved in the event. Myorr would always give me a thousand dollar chip for my birthday to gamble with. Getting a thousand dollars for my birthday was beyond a regular gift. I never told Myorr I kept it instead of gambling. I felt that when you gamble at the Black Jack table or in life, there's always a chance you would loose it all.

Myorr was always making sure I was okay. He was beyond a boss. He never really understood that I admired him for not only the way he was on the clock for Russell, but I admired him for his heart and the loyalty he had with his mother, his fiancé Serci, and his friends. A lot of people said I was kissing his you-know-what, but I wasn't. I was genuinely respecting my boss and admiring a role model.

Between 2005 and 2006 I was all over Russell's national ads modeling Phat Farm. I was only 26-years-old. We were on another Phat Farm Tour traveling all over the world. At this point I was doing public relations, working with certain stylists on their magazine photo shoots, traveling with Russell and Myorr promoting Phat Farm on a 30-city tour, modeling, and taking acting classes in NYC. My life was extremely busy. I had no time for friends, family, or even for myself. My escape was working out with Russell and Rev. Run in the mornings at our hotel gyms or tagging along with Russell to do yoga. I had to find a way to make it to the gym to keep my body in shape. At this point my waist was 33 inches, so I could fit in all the samples at photo shoots effortlessly.

One day I was running around with Steve Lobel in L.A. and he introduced me to Jessy Terrero and Uly Terrero, also known as the Terrero brothers. Jessy is a director for movies, commercials, and music videos and his brother Uly is a casting director for commercials, movies, and music videos. I made a close friendship with them and they always invited me to different video shoots and movie sets they were working on. Jessy always kept me in mind for videos to play as an extra for him. Like when he directed a video for P. Diddy's girl group, Dream, he hit me up on the Blackberry asking me to play the part of one of the girl's boyfriends in the video, but I wasn't able to cause I was with Russell traveling.

Uly always kept me in mind when he was casting for a commercial and movie auditions. Because of Uly I auditioned for so many roles. I landed a role as the third lead actor for a movie that Adam Yauch from the Beastie Boys was putting together. I audition about five times for this role. There must have been about 100 guys all auditioning for the same role. I got the role, but there was a conflict with Adam's schedule so it never happened. I didn't take it personal. That's the business—it happens.

When Russell and Rev. Run were doing a Phat Farm in-store signing in Orlando, Florida, the best part about it was my family lived only two-hours away. I made sure my family was aware of us coming down there so they could come out and see me. It's an amazing feeling when you get to see your family after a year and a half of only speaking to them over the phone. But what's really amazing was when they got to really see what I did for a living, meet my bosses, and spend time with me while I worked.

The in-store signing started at 3 p.m. As the radio disc jockey was promoting Russell and Rev's presence to the Orlando area over the radio, my goddaughter/

niece Thalia tackled me. She screamed, "Tio Kari [Uncle Kari]!" I was in shock. As I'm hugging her, I look up and see the woman of my life—my mother. I couldn't help the tear that came down my eye when I saw my mother. The look on her face was a memorable one as she smiled and hugged me. You see, the only thing I could think of at this time was Cheyenne, my father, and all the struggling and sacrifices these two men put my mother through. I wanted her to see she still had a son that hadn't given up on her and life itself. I kissed her forehead and told her I loved her.

My mother grabbed my face and said, "Son, I love you. I've missed you, and I'm so proud of you."

How could I not cry hearing my mother say that? I cried and wiped my face quickly to hide it from everyone in the store.

Then I hugged my sister Yassina, Yazmin, my brother-in-law Yobanny and my little nieces and nephew. I introduced my family to Myorr and they all felt like they have known him for years because I spoke about him so much. Myorr spoke to my family and told them how happy he was having me as part of the company. I then introduced them to Russell and Rev. Run while they are at the table signing autographs. Of course Russell said a joke about me. He said that my family was beautiful and asked what happened to me.

My oldest sister Yassina came up to me after all the emotions were let out. She hugged my waist and said, "Baby bro, I am so freaking proud of you. I can't believe how long you have come. You deserve this one hundred percent. It's so amazing how you have overcome all the stuff you've been through. You had Cheyenne's shadow to walk in, but look at you; you did all this on your own, kid. Beyond and bigger than Cheyenne. I mean, Russell and Rev. Run are signing at a store and your face is all over the place on display at the store, promoting Phat Farm."

After the in-store signing I told my family to come down to my hotel and hang out with me. We pulled up to the Ritz Carlton five-star hotel and it was actually funny seeing my family all getting out of an old family van pulled up behind our rented black Yukon Denali. I made fun of my sister and told her the "hillbillies" are in town. My sister just laughed with me and hugged me.

Myorr and I checked Russell and the rest of the Phat Farm crew into our hotel rooms. Myorr asked me where my family was staying. I explained that they were going back home later tonight unless they wanted to stay with me in my room. Myorr handed me two different sets of keys.

I asked, "What's this?"

"One room is for you and your mom, the other room is for your sisters, the kids and her husband."

I looked at Myorr in shock. I was speechless.

I hugged him and said, "Thank you, man."

"No problem, man. Catch up with your mom and family."

For the first time in their lives they were able to know what it feels like to stay in a five-star hotel.

I will always remember what Myorr did for me that night because he didn't have to buy them a room for me. He took care of my family. Thank you, Myorr.

In 2006 and there was a major concert called Live 8. Every major musician, actor and artist from Stevie Wonder to Jay Z, from Alicia Keys, to Richard Gere was there. Russell was asked to be a part of the incredible event, so I went with him to work with Jody Miller, his other publicist. As the concert was going on, Jody Miller and I were moving Russell from tent to tent, making sure he was being interviewed at all the news stands for TV and print. I met every celebrity I possibly could and gave them my business card so I could send them Phat Farm clothing in appreciation from Russell; it was our way of getting free marketing on celebrities. I even took a photo with Richard Gere, just for my mom because she loved him and was obsessed with his movie *Pretty Woman.*

After I said "what's up" to Lincoln Park, I ran over to Alicia Keys's trailer to say "hello" with Russell and while we were there I was talking to Onree Gill, composer, producer, and musical director for Alicia Keys. It's crazy because I used to see this guy with her onstage all the time performing with her. Onree and I talked for almost an hour and after I gave him my business card, I thought it would be a great opportunity to ask him if he would want to work with me on a song. Onree responded, "Yeah man, no doubt. Hit me up when you get down time and we'll figure out a good day and time to work." I didn't know if Onree was just saying this to just say it because I was with Russell, but I took down his information and told him I would follow up.

About two weeks later I was sending out packages of clothes to all the musicians and celebrities from the Live 8 concert for Russell. I came across Onree's information, so I put together a nice big box of clothes and sneakers for him. I sent him a text on the Blackberry letting him know he had a package coming his way. He responded with, "Thanks! So, when are we getting you to my studio so we can work on a new song?"

I was shocked he remembered! So I said, "Let's do this, man!"

I ended up at his studio that weekend and we started working together. I met his family, we talked and I let him get to know me and how influenced I was by music and what my goals were with this project. At first I wanted to be famous as a singer, I wanted to touch the world with my voice and words. I didn't want my listeners to just listen to my songs, I wanted them to feel like they were right there with me singing it, feeling it, and loving it.

Onree is an incredible producer, one of the very few that could make a beat for me from scratch in only a couple hours. So, the way we did it was Onree created the beat from nothing, but just the theme I wanted. As Onree is working on the beat, I was writing the lyrics and by the end of the night we had a song produced, written, and recorded all together. This routine worked every time. I made a personal friendship with Onree, so every time we met up it was at 10 a.m., started working at 11 a.m. and we stayed working on a song till 1 or 2 a.m. I would always go home with a rough draft song or a song mastered—a song created in just hours. I would get home around 3 a.m., go to bed till 4:30 a.m., get up and hit the gym again, then run back to New York, so I could be at Phat Farm before the bosses.

I always kept in the back of my head what P.Diddy said, "Karim, sleep when you are dead."

Of course with Onree's crazy schedule and my hectic schedule, we didn't get to record as often as I wanted, but Onree loved working with me so we ended up going from one song to a lot more. Onree and I kept close communication and friendship. I follow his work till this day and always keep him and his family in my prayers.

One time after a long week of traveling and going to four different cities in a matter of three days, we landed in Teterboro Airport, NJ at the private airport. I was sitting across from Russell, "T", the president to Russell's new record label sat right next to Russell, Myorr sat right next to me, and the rest of the commission sat in the rear of the plane still sleeping. I was looking out the window with my headphones and Ipod on. I started singing an R&B song by R. Kelly under my breath that reminded me of my brother, as I was looking outside the window, watching the airport employees run around getting things together and ready for us while we landed.

Russell slapped my leg and said, "Yo, what you singing?"

I said, "A song by R. Kelly."

"Sing that louder! Let me hear you."

So as I started singing, the butterflies and knots began. I started thinking in the back of my mind how amazing this moment was because when I was an intern my goal was to be able to sing to Russell. I knew if there was any person in the world that knows talent it was definitely The Godfather of Hip Hop.

Russell cut me off, "Yo, sing another one." He had this look of amazement on his face.

So I started singing another song. I pictured my brother Cheyenne there singing with me. I felt more comfortable. It was like finally Cheyenne and I had the chance to display our talent. Russell still looked amazed.

"Yo, this kid got soul! Where did this come from? I'm blown away. A Latino with soul!"

I stopped singing.

He said, "Yo, man, I didn't know you could sing."

He turned to his record label president "T" and said, "Yo, get him in the studio! I need to get him recorded!"

Then "T" looked at me and said, "Yea, but can you write your own lyrics?"

I replied, "Yes."

Later on I gave my luggage to my driver who picked me up from the airport. I rode home with tears in my eyes, thanking God. I was excited that my goal of getting to sing to Russell finally came true! I looked to my right while I was sitting in the back of the car while the driver was driving me home and I saw Cheyenne with tears of excitement in his eyes.

Unfortunately "T" never fulfilled Russell's request. He never asked me to go to the studio, never called me, never followed through to get me a beat or anything. Every time I called "T" his excuse was, "I got you, Karim, soon as I get a chance." I never heard from him. I didn't want to annoy Russell because he had so many other things going on so I just let it ride out. I guess it just wasn't meant to be. But that doesn't mean anything except it just wasn't meant to be with Russell's record label at that time. I went back to the studio with Onree Gill and kept writing and recording. Regardless of what didn't happen with "T", there came a day that I needed to sit down and talk with Myorr, not from a co-worker to his boss, but as a little brother to a big brother.

Myorr saw in my face there was something serious I wanted to talk about so he hung up his phone and asked me if I was okay.

"Yea, man, everything is good."

"What's up, Karim?"

"Myorr I wanted to know your opinion on something. I have been modeling for a couple years and acting on the side and working on my album as well. I've been getting hit up from agents in L.A. to work with them and I feel like I'm at the point that I have hit a glass ceiling here at Phat Farm. I don't want Russell to think I'm not loyal to him in anyway, but I think I need to try and extend my horizons and move to L.A. for a little while and try out the L.A. lifestyle. I know I can't take a leave of absence, so I wanted to know what did you think? Am I making a big mistake by wanting to leave Phat Farm to try something new?"

"Karim, you know I love you like family. If I were you, at your age, and making the contacts you have made here over the past years. I would probably leave too. Karim, you're young and have so much going on for you. The worst feeling in the world is if you don't leave, you will always wonder 'what if.' I think you should try it out man. Worse case scenario, if it doesn't work, you come back to New York City and if we are hiring, I'll bring you back. If we aren't hiring, I'm sure you'll find another job doing public relations for another great company."

I hugged Myorr and thanked him for all his guidance and support throughout the years. Most of all I thanked him for being a mentor to me, and most of all for being real, like a big brother to me.

Here I was walking with butterflies in my stomach and knots causing a sweat on my face. As I'm on the elevator going 40 floors down to the street level, I started reminiscing on how five and a half years later I am on the same elevator and with the same knots and nervous feeling I had when Russell called me to his car to hire me. Yet here I am now going to speak with him and give him news that he's not aware of.

I exited the elevator and walked past the security guards at the elevator. I heard them say, "Hello, Mr. Ramos," but I was just so focused and nervous on what was about to happen, that I didn't even respond to the guards.

I walk out to 7th Avenue in the front of our building. I got a flash back and saw that intern walking to Russell's car, not knowing what the boss was going to say five and a half years ago. I had my thoughts all over the place in my head. I didn't know if Russell was going to support my feelings and decision, or if he was going to be disappointed in me. My hands grabbed the handle to his Maybach car and I shut the door after I got in—silence.

Everything I was thinking was gone. My mind went blank till Russell said, "What's up, Karim?"

"Russ, what's up man?" It all came back to me. "Hey, so I've been thinking a lot and I just spoke to Myorr about this. Basically, I want to first thank you for all the life lessons you have taught me. For making me see that being humble and helping those in need are some things we as people should practice daily. Russell, I am here today to ask for your blessing. I have decided to leave Phat Farm to try and pursue my love for music as an artist or even just a writer, some acting and modeling on the west coast for a little while.

"I am torn because you and Myorr gave me a shot when this Puerto Rican kid came to you guys over five years ago needing a chance to show you that I can make a difference in your empire without a college degree. You didn't judge me for what degrees or experience I had in the fashion business. You took a shot in the dark and went with your gut.

"Russell, I love you and thank you for all the opportunities you have given me. Most of all I thank you for the love you have given me back and just ask that before I leave this car, I will still have family here at Phat Fashions . . . that you will still keep a friendship with me. You guys were my family for years and being I don't have family here, I grew up in this family."

Russell said, "Karim, you will always have a family here. If you need anything from me here or on the west coast, please let me know."

And just like that, the conversation was done. The Phat Train was over.

I got out of the car and headed back to Penn Station to take my train to go home. As I was walking back to the train, I started to get flash backs. I couldn't hear the noisy city anymore. I wasn't that intern that was blown away from the people screaming and yelling, the lights, the buildings, and the cars. Every step I took toward the train station seemed like a step to the unknown land of Karim Ramos. Not knowing what to expect tomorrow morning I risked a lifetime career for something I wanted to try to pursue. Just like when I left Ocala, FL with nothing on me—the fat country kid that took his mom's old car to follow his heart in New York with nothing but a dream and hope to make it in New York City.

I arrived at Penn Station and looked over my shoulder and smiled at New York City. The city that doesn't care where you are, where you're going, or what you want. The city that doesn't sleep but she watches you everyday and doesn't even acknowledge your feelings. She will destroy you if you are not on your "A" game. New York has made many famous and destroyed many. I felt I won the battle of Karim vs. New York. The industry took this corny, chubby kid and transformed him to a man with pride, humbleness, loyalty, a positive attitude, thankfulness, and most of all it made me a believer in myself.

Going from the Fat kid to the Phat kid was an experience I realized would have never happened if I didn't believe in God, take risks, really motivate myself, love myself, and appreciate the talents given to me and the talents I had to discover within myself. I was confused when my parents got divorced when I was 13-years-old. I was misguided when I lost my relationship with my father. I lost hope when I buried my only brother. I lost faith when I was waking up on a park bench on an empty stomach with no food, no blanket, no one to cry to, not knowing if I died tomorrow would I be missed? Thinking like my brother did, saying suicide was the best answer.

When you feel the world is against you, it's kind of hard to believe in yourself. My tears and fears I faced, no one will ever know, but I hope and pray my tears, fears, failures, accomplishment, and success will motivate you as a reader to realize that we all have a story to tell about ourselves. I just hope my story will motivate you and inspire you to know you are not alone. I am no different then you, we all have our downfalls and tragedies. Believe in yourself! Remember the past so you may grow, just don't dwell in the things you can't change, that's how life is. The main thing you have to tell yourself is the same things I tell myself till this day. No matter how many people want to see you fail, no matter how hard life is, no matter how alone you feel, no matter how impossible your goals seem, take that step of faith, put God first and do not fear change.

I really had to master the word "hustler", which in my eyes means someone who does what they have to do (with respect to themselves and others and with a positive attitude) to get what they want. I wanted to be like Myorr, a marketing guru who was respected and loved by everyone and humble at what he did. I wanted to be like Russell, music and fashion mogul serving his own companies, fans, supporters and motivating the un-motivated. I wanted to be like Rev. Run, a man who lived his life by always placing God first and preaching the word of God daily to his friends and family. Then I wanted to be a famous model to motivate myself, my family, my friends, and even my enemies. I wanted to get a call from my family saying that they saw my picture in a magazine, or they walked passed a billboard and saw me, or even on a commercial.

I want my mother and father to see that even though they had a son that killed himself they never at any moment failed as parents. We all have a gift, the gift of life. We all have a choice, to choose the right or wrong path of life. I want my brother Cheyenne to know that till this day I admire who he was and that if he's looking down on me, I hope he is proud of his baby brother. Our past should only make us stronger and better. If there's anything I have learned from my mistakes and the mistakes of others is that our mistakes give us a story to tell to help others, but learn from them and continue to grow and get what you want out of life. The number one rule to be able to get what you want is to NEVER GIVE UP!

CHAPTER 10

Health & Fitness Come First

Good nutrition is the cornerstone to good health. What you put in is what you get out, and having a healthy and well balanced diet not only affects the way you look, it also affects the way you feel. The foods you eat play a role in how much you weigh, your energy level, the aging process, how often you get sick (immune system), and even your risk of chronic diseases such as heart disease, diabetes, obesity, and certain types of cancer.

I know this now, but coming from an overweight kid who grew up on Oreo cookies and Fruit Loop cereal, nutrition was not always at the top of my priority list. Let's face it, eating healthy isn't always easy. Did you ever think about why you eat? Well the obvious answer is because you are hungry, but emotions also play a big role in our decision to eat. Have you ever craved chicken soup when you were sick or cookies when you were feeling depressed. Does the thought of an ice cream sundae remind you of being a kid again? There are many reasons besides hunger that drive us to eat such as boredom, sadness, anxiety, feeling like we don't want to waste food, because it is lunchtime, and even because eating is associated with a particular event like popcorn and movies or peanuts and baseball games.

For me, even as a young child, eating helped me deal with my emotions. Let me start from the beginning. When I was a baby, I weighed over ten pounds. I ate a lot, and that habit lasted right into my teenage years as the pounds just kept creeping up. Even though I was an active kid, I was also a very hungry kid. I literally wiped clean every plate my mother ever served me. I loved candy, cookies, donuts, and muffins; heck, I liked anything sweet! By the time I was twenty years old, I was at my highest weight. I had a double chin, love handles, and practically no self confidence. My clothes just kept getting baggier as I gained more weight. I figured I could hide under the big clothes, but who was I kidding. I couldn't hide from myself. I was insecure, lonely, and very depressed. I started to not care about anything. I didn't care about my grades in school, my friends, sports, and most importantly, I didn't care about myself. I was at my lowest point, and I needed to make a change.

My big brother passing away was the turning point in my life. Looking at him lying in that coffin gave me the motivation to want to better my life. My brother was handsome, lean, and athletic. I wanted to be just like him. I wanted to make him proud. I was tired of being just some fat kid. YOU have to find what motivates you. Whatever it might be that motivates you, you have to find it, grab onto it, and hold on tight because being healthy is a lifelong journey. You will have bumps along the way and you might take a few wrong turns, but as long as you get back on the road to good health, it will be worth the ride.

When I finally decided to change my life, I weighed 262lbs and was at 42% body fat. Where was I even going to begin? My gym was offering a boot camp class, so I decided to join. I went to the gym faithfully, every morning for an hour of cardio and calisthenics. I lost 30 pounds in 2 months, but that was just the beginning for me. I had a lot more to go. The pounds just kept dropping off, and that kept me motivated to keep at it. After a few months, I hit a plateau, and the weight stopped dropping. I needed to do something different. My body was getting used to my workouts and stopped responding, so I needed to change things up. I began going to the gym twice a day; cardio in the morning and weights in the evening. I read so many articles and studies that said you need at least 25 minutes of cardio a day to burn fat, so I made sure I was doing 45-60 minutes a day of cardio plus an hour of weight training. Although this was pretty intense, I was determined to lose the weight.

Working out will be hard for the first month since it will be new for you. Your body will be sore, you might feel tired, and you might even think about giving up. That is when you have to find that source of motivation again. That is when you have to reflect on the reasons why you are doing this. What motivates YOU? Remember, Rome wasn't built in one day, so don't give up. Stay focused and if you fall off track, get up, dust yourself off, and get right back on! It will take a lot of work and dedication to get the goal you want, but your health and happiness is worth it. 90% of the way your body looks is what YOU EAT, and what you put in is what you get out. You can work out for hours, but if you don't eat right, you won't look or feel right!

Here are a few tips to help you along the way

Eat Breakfast—Ever heard that breakfast is the most important meal of the day? Well, it's true. When people miss breakfast, they miss more than just a meal. Research shows that starting your day off with a healthy breakfast helps with calorie control for the rest of the day. This is because breakfast jump-starts your metabolism—helping prevent those mid-morning snack attacks and unhealthy binges that can sabotage a healthy weight. Studies also show that breakfast eaters tend to have more strength and endurance plus better concentration and problem-solving abilities. On the flip side, those who skip breakfast often feel tired, irritable or restless in the morning.

Breakfast should be a combination of healthy carbohydrates, protein and a small amount of healthy fat. Here are a few ideas:

Whole grain cold cereal, berries, low-fat milk
Whole grain English muffin with low fat cream cheese and a glass of
  orange juice
Smoothie: low fat milk, banana, low fat yogurt and a scoop of peanut
  butter
Whole grain oatmeal, chopped walnuts and raisins
Frozen whole-grain waffles with cup of yogurt and your favorite fruit
Whole-grain breakfast wrap with turkey and low-fat cheese

Watch Portion Sizes—ever heard the expression, "everything in moderation?" You can enjoy most foods as long as you don't overdo it. Besides when you deprive yourself of foods you love, you often end up binging on them later.

Back to the Basics—aim for natural, unprocessed foods such as fruits, vegetables, whole grains, low fat dairy and lean meat and seafood.

Go vegan at least once a week—beans are a great source of protein as well as fiber and other important vitamins and minerals. Try a three bean chili instead of using the traditional ground beef

Avoid Liquid Calories—soda, sugary beverages and alcohol can all wreck havoc on your waistline. WATER, WATER, WATER, the more the better. If you need a little flavor, squeeze in a lemon, lime or orange.

Trust your intuition—as babies, we cried when we were hungry and stopped eating when we were full, regardless of what was left on our plate. As we become adults, we convert to what I call the "clean plate club." We feel the need to finish everything on our plates, even if we are already full. Stop eating before you feel "stuffed." And eat slowly. It takes your body 20 minutes to register fullness, so eating fast will cause you to overeat.

Here are a few tips that can help:

1. Create a healthful lifestyle, not just a "diet." Though it may be tempting to follow the latest fad diet, it's likely the results won't last. Instead, stick to the cornerstones of healthful eating and physical activity.

2. Think nutrient-rich rather than "good" or "bad." No single food or meal makes or breaks a healthful diet. So look at the big picture. Your total diet is the key to healthful eating. The majority of your food choices should be packed with vitamins, minerals, fiber and other nutrients—and low in fat, cholesterol, sodium and sugar.

3. Add more whole grains to your diet. Set a goal to make half of your grains whole grains each day. Choose whole-grain pantry staples such as whole-grain pasta, brown rice and whole-wheat bread.

4. Read food labels. They'll help you make smart food choices quickly and easily. Rely on food labels to show nutritional values as well as list ingredients in descending order by amount. Be sure to check the serving size, remember that calories count, and choose foods low in saturated fat, trans fat, sodium and sugar.

5. Choose healthy fats. Look for polyunsaturated or monounsaturated fats (like olive oil or canola oil), and keep your saturated fats, trans fats and cholesterol intake low.

6. Get moving! Balancing physical activity and a healthful diet is your best recipe for managing weight and promoting overall health and fitness.

7. Eat more fruits and veggies. The majority of Americans are not eating enough fruits and vegetables. Fruits and vegetables contain powerful disease fighting antioxidants, as well as essential vitamins and minerals

8. Drink your milk. Your mother was right. It's important to drink milk every day. Milk is an important source of calcium, vitamin D and protein. Choose low fat or fat free milk.

9. Prepare meals at home. You have more control over how your food is prepared and which ingredients are used.

10. Pack it—don't wait for hunger pains to think about what you are going to eat. When you are starving, you are more likely to choose something unhealthy. Be prepared and pack your healthy meals and snacks.

A few more . . . .

- Control portions and eat from a plate, not out of a package.
- Eat slowly and put your fork down between bites. This allows your body to recognize fullness.
- Don't pick. Contrary to what we'd like to believe: sips, tastes, bites, foods that crumble, foods that don't hit your plate, food you eat while standing up, or the remainder of your child's lunch do in fact have calories and can add up quickly.
- Make eating the only event and enjoy it. When you eat while watching T.V., you may consume more than you think.
- Go food shopping on a full stomach and stick to a shopping list.
- When you're not really hungry but you get the urge to nibble out of boredom or stress, do something else like read, take a walk, watch television, or call a friend.
- Keep portions in check since even healthy food can result in weight gain if you eat more than you should. For example, two cups of brown rice, yes even brown rice, is still around 500 calories. Try measuring your portions for about a week to make sure you are eating appropriate amounts.
- Exercise is not a license to overeat. It takes 30 minutes to burn around 200-300 calories, and 1 minute to eat 2 cookies for the same amount of calories.
- Hunger is a symptom of fatigue, so it is common to remedy your sleepiness with eating. Plus, when you are tired your judgment may be impaired and you are less likely to care about planning healthy meals. Make it a priority to get an adequate amount of sleep each night.

Overweight Teen

My Senior High School Picture

KARIM RAMOS

My Head Shot

Head Shot

215lbs to 187lbs on my strict diet and hard training
Thanks, Nick Freglette

215lbs to 187lbs on my strict diet and hard training
Thanks, Nick Freglette